Microsoft

Ed Bott's Your New PC: Seven Easy Steps to Help You Get Started!

Ed Bott

PUBLISHED BY
Microsoft Press
A Division of Microsoft Corporation
One Microsoft Way
Redmond, Washington 98052-6399

Library of Congress Control Number 2004111490

Printed and bound in the United States of America.

3 4 5 6 7 8 9   QWT   9 8 7 6 5 4

Distributed in Canada by H.B. Fenn and Company Ltd.

A CIP catalogue record for this book is available from the British Library.

Microsoft Press books are available through booksellers and distributors worldwide. For further information about international editions, contact your local Microsoft Corporation office or contact Microsoft Press International directly at fax (425) 936-7329. Visit our Web site at www.microsoft.com/ learning/. Send comments to *mspinput@microsoft.com*.

ActiveSync, ActiveX, Hotmail, Microsoft, Microsoft Press, MSN, Outlook, PowerPoint, Windows, Windows Media, and Windows Mobile are either registered trademarks or trademarks of Microsoft Corporation in the United States and/or other countries.

The example companies, organizations, products, domain names, e-mail addresses, logos, people, places, and events depicted herein are fictitious. No association with any real company, organization, product, domain name, e-mail address, logo, person, place, or event is intended or should be inferred.

This book expresses the author's views and opinions. The information contained in this book is provided without any express, statutory, or implied warranties. Neither the authors, Microsoft Corporation, nor its resellers or distributors will be held liable for any damages caused or alleged to be caused either directly or indirectly by this book.

Acquisitions Editor: Alex Blanton
Project Editor: Devon Musgrave
Indexer: Patricia Masserman

Body Part No. X10-87061

Contents

Step 4

Move Files and Settings   108

Step 5

Set Up Printers, Digital Cameras, and Other Hardware   128

Step 6

Instant Productivity: Just Add Software   152

Introduction

So, you've got a new PC. Now what?

After you take the pieces out of the box, the fun begins—but so does the work. How do you make sure your new PC is protected from viruses, spyware, and hackers? How do you get your e-mail messages, your address book, and your collection of digital music off your old PC and onto the new one? What do you do with all the programs on your old computer? How do you create a home network with your old computer and your new one? Why don't your old printer and scanner work anymore?

Good questions. And if you don't know the answers, you've got lots of company.

Over the past few years, I've installed more than two dozen new PCs for friends, family members, and neighbors. I help them shop for the best deals, unpack the new computers and set them up, update Windows, configure their security options, move the data and settings from their old PCs, and guide them through the process of installing programs and setting up e-mail. By the time I leave, they can be confident they're not going to run into any startup glitches, and they're ready to get to work (or start playing their favorite games).

Unfortunately, I can't personally visit your home and help you set up your new PC. So I've done the next best thing: I wrote this book. The purpose of *Ed Bott's Your New PC* is to show you, step by step, how to set up your new computer the right way. This book represents exactly what I do when I put together a new PC for my dad, or my real estate agent Dorothy, or my neighbor Jerry.

I make a few assumptions about you and your new PC in this book. I assume your new computer has Microsoft Windows XP installed on it. I figure you've probably used a computer for several years already and you understand the basics of pointing, clicking, and browsing the Web, so I won't waste your time with unnecessary tutorials. Oh, and if your computer isn't exactly brand new, that's OK. Even if you've been using your PC for several months, you can still use the advice in this book to make sure that your "gently used" PC is secure and that your data and settings are well-organized.

How to Read This Book

When I sit alongside a friend or neighbor and help them set up their new computer, I follow a simple, seven-step program. This book is organized the same way. I wrote this book to be read in order, from front to back; you can literally check off each task on the list as you complete it. Many steps assume you've already accomplished an earlier task; if you try to skip around, you risk missing an important prerequisite.

Before you dive in, I want you to read the short chapter "Before You Begin." In it, I explain what you need to do before you start plugging in hardware and installing software. Follow the advice I lay out here, and you won't find yourself stuck later when you're asked to produce a missing disk or type in a password you can't remember.

If you're experienced with Windows and are impatient—or if you just want an overview of the seven-step process—read "The Short Version," beginning on page 14. This is the pedal-to-the-metal routine I follow when I'm setting up a new PC. You'll find all the steps here, in quick, summary fashion, without a lot of detail. You can skip this chapter if you want all the details of all seven steps.

With those preliminaries out of the way, you're ready to get started. Each step of the actual process gets its own chapter, starting with "Step 1: Out of the Box." Each chapter begins with a short introduction that succinctly explains why this step is necessary and what you as the reader will accomplish. You'll find the following common elements in all seven of the numbered chapters:

- A **checklist** at the beginning of the chapter that identifies each task you need to complete. Each item on the list corresponds to a heading and section in the chapter. See the check box to the left? When you've completed each task, check it off and move on.

- **Notes** and **Tips** that explain important details about specific tasks. I've written this book in plain English, with a minimum of technobabble. Tips, in particular, represent time-saving shortcuts I've discovered over the years.

- When you see a **Caution**, pay attention! That identifies a place where I think you can get into trouble if you try to move too quickly or take a shortcut.

In the final chapter, "Clean Up Your Old Computer," I share my advice on what to do with your old PC after you get the new one up and running. For starters, don't just throw it in the dump—you don't have to look hard to find a responsible recycling option instead. And be sure to wipe out sensitive files on the old PC before you give it away.

A Word about Windows

As I mentioned earlier, I assume your new PC already has Windows XP installed on it. In the course of this book, you'll see a lot of discussion about Windows XP Service Pack 2 (better known as SP2). This update to Windows XP was released in August 2004, and it includes an enormous number of changes to the operating system. In particular, it adds security features that go a long way toward protecting your PC—and you—from threats on the Internet. Your copy of Windows XP may already be updated with SP2, or you may have an earlier version of Windows. In my opinion, making sure that SP2 is correctly installed on your computer is the single most important step you can take to increase your PC's security. Be sure you follow these instructions to the letter.

Acknowledgments

I've wanted to write this book for years, and I'm grateful to the people who made it possible. At Microsoft Press, Alex Blanton convinced the right people to say yes, Devon Musgrave and Sandra Haynes did the heavy editorial lifting, and Carl Diltz turned the words into pages. Jim Kramer did the book design, Joel Panchot is responsible for the most excellent illustrations, and Patricia Masserman assembled the index. Claudette Moore and Debbie McKenna of Moore Literary Agency did what they do so well—keeping track of the business details so I can concentrate on these pesky PCs. Thanks to my many friends and neighbors who have pestered me with PC questions over the years, making this book not only possible nut necessary. And above all, a heartfelt thanks to my wife Judy, whose love and support is priceless.

Microsoft Learning Technical Support

Every effort has been made to ensure the accuracy of this book. Microsoft Press provides corrections for books through the World Wide Web at *http://www.microsoft.com/learning/support/*. To connect directly to the Microsoft Knowledge Base and enter a query regarding a question or issue, go to *http://www.microsoft.com/learning/support/search.asp*. If you have comments, questions, or ideas regarding this book, please send them to Microsoft Press using either of the following methods:

Microsoft Press Attn: *Ed Bott's Your New PC* Editor
One Microsoft Way
Redmond, WA 98052-6399
mspinput@microsoft.com

Before You Begin

Wouldn't it be nice if setting up a personal computer were just a matter of plugging it in and turning it on? Well, we can dream, can't we? Your new PC is a marvel of modern technology, but it should come as no surprise that you'll need to take care of a lot of little tasks—and a few big ones—to get everything running right.

You could just dive in, fire up Microsoft Windows XP, and begin pointing, clicking, and configuring. The trouble with that head-first strategy is that you'll quickly find yourself stuck when you can't figure out whether the speaker connector goes in the green jack or the blue one. Or when Windows demands a CD that you haven't seen for months. Or when you're asked to enter a password and you haven't the slightest idea what to type.

I can help you keep from getting stuck midway between your old PC and your new one. If you take just a little time now to gather the things you'll need later—program disks, drivers for your hardware, e-mail passwords, and network settings—you should sail through this book.

☑ Checklist:

❏ **Get your new computer (page 4).** Your new PC can come from a big-name mail-order house, from a local techie, or from your own garage. In this book, I assume you've assembled all the hardware you need and that Windows XP (Home Edition or Professional) is installed.

❏ **Round up your hardware manuals and driver disks (page 6).** You may need the manual to figure out exactly what each port on the back of the PC does. Driver disks help Windows communicate with your hardware and are especially important for printers and scanners.

❏ **Locate your Windows CD and product key (page 6).** You probably won't need these pieces right away, but it's good to keep them in a safe place.

❏ **Gather your program disks (page 8).** There's no easy way to transfer programs from your old PC to your new one. Along with the CDs, you may need serial numbers, product keys, and installation instructions as well.

❏ **Collect your downloaded programs (page 9).** Some of your favorite programs are probably scattered in various location on your hard disk. Get them together now and you won't need to download fresh copies later.

❏ **Print out your Internet and e-mail settings (page 11).** Do you have a broadband connection? Ask your Internet service provider if you need to do anything special to connect your new PC. Make a note of user names, passwords, server names, and other settings for your e-mail accounts.

❏ **Make a note of your network settings (page 13).** Windows does all the work if your network is simple. You'll need to gather some extra details if you have a broadband router, a corporate network connection, a print server, or any wireless equipment.

Get your new computer

Before you can follow the advice in this book, you'll need a new PC. I suppose this should go without saying—after all, this book is called *Ed Bott's Your New PC*, right? But not all new PCs are created equal, and how you follow the advice in this book depends, to a great extent, on where your new PC comes from.

Which of the following descriptions best fits your new PC?

- **A name-brand computer, purchased from a retail store or by mail order.** Big-name PC makers sell computers by the millions, and that allows them to forge special relationships with Microsoft and other software makers. When you buy a new computer from one of these companies—such as Dell, Hewlett-Packard, Sony, or IBM—you'll find that the version of Windows XP installed on the computer has been customized to add the manufacturer's logo and links to its Web site in various places. (Figure 1 shows custom content in the Help and Support Center on a Toshiba notebook.) In addition, you'll probably find that extra programs have been preinstalled for you. When you first turn on the computer, you'll probably run through a simple setup program before you get to the Windows desktop.

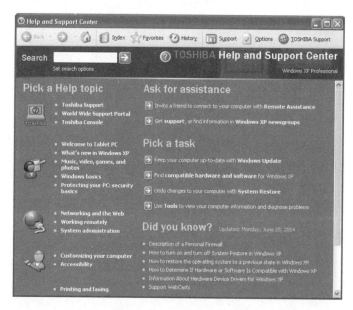

Figure 1 *An example of custom content on a name-brand computer.*

- **A custom PC, built by a local computer store or a small mail-order vendor.**
  Unlike their name-brand counterparts, these no-name computers (sometimes
  referred to as "white box" PCs) aren't extensively customized. Typically, they
  use a standard version of Windows that original equipment manufacturers
  (OEMs) buy at a discount over the boxed version you'll find in the software
  section of your local computer emporium. You can count on the computer
  maker to install drivers for all the hardware in your new computer, but you
  won't typically find any extra software preinstalled unless you specifically
  ordered it.

- **A do-it-yourself project.** You don't need to be a rocket scientist to build your
  own PC. If you can use a screwdriver and follow instructions, you can put
  together a PC from scratch. Some stores sell "bare bones" systems that include
  the basic computer components and allow you to add your own memory,
  hard disk, and other components. You'll also need to purchase an OEM or
  retail copy of Windows XP and install it, along with any necessary hardware
  drivers and utilities. If you choose this option, I assume you know how to
  format your hard disk and install Windows (or you can find the expert help
  you need to get past this step).

- **A gently used, upgraded PC.** If your computer is reasonably new, you might
  want to start over—or you might need to reformat your hard disk and reinstall
  Windows XP to recover from a virus infection or a hard disk crash. Technically,
  your upgraded PC isn't new, but you can treat it as if it were new. By following
  the advice in this book, you can make sure your old hardware and freshly
  installed software are working in perfect harmony.

And what if you've been using your new PC for a few weeks or months? Have no
fear. Although the advice in this book was written with the assumption that you're
starting from scratch, you'll find plenty of ways to make your almost-but-not-quite-
new PC faster and more secure—and to help yourself become better organized and
more productive.

☐ Round up your hardware manuals and driver disks

Long ago, manuals for computer hardware were as thick as encyclopedias. Today's manuals are slim, and usually they contain just the basic information you need to set up, configure, and troubleshoot the device in question. If your PC's manufacturer has done things properly, you won't need the manuals. But it's handy to have them around so that you can look up details like which audio jack is for your speakers and which is for your microphone.

In addition, your new PC probably came with an assortment of CDs that contain drivers and utility programs for your hardware. As you work through the nitty-gritty of getting everything connected, you might find that you need one or more of those disks. So keep them close at hand.

Of course, if you need special access software or hardware drivers to access the Internet, make sure you have those files on hand *before* you start setting up your new PC. If necessary, download the latest software using your old PC, because you won't be able to download anything on your new PC until that software is up and running!

TIP   Right now would be a good time to put together a system for keeping track of *all* the disks and documents associated with your new PC. I use inexpensive expanding envelopes, made from clear plastic, which seal up with a string. I buy them by the dozen at my local office-supply store and use two or three to store receipts, packing slips, setup instructions, CDs, manuals, and scraps of paper on which I've written useful information, like serial numbers. I then store the envelopes in a safe place within arm's reach of the PC. Later, if I need to look up a detail about my PC or reinstall a piece of software from the original CD, I know exactly where to find it.

☐ Locate your Windows CD and product key

If your new PC came with Windows XP already installed, why do you need the Windows CD? For now, you probably don't. But you'll need it if you want to install some of the optional components on the CD—notably the Backup program (see page 197 for details). You'll also need the original Windows XP CD if you ever have to reinstall or repair Windows for any reason. Put it in a safe place now, along with the Certificate of Authenticity and other paperwork that came with the CD.

You'll also want to make sure you keep your Windows XP *product key* handy. This is the 25-character code you need to type in before you can run the Windows Setup program from CD. (Figure 2 shows the screen you'll encounter when you run Setup.) If you purchased a retail (boxed) copy of Windows XP, the product key is probably printed on a sticker attached to the back of the CD case. If your new PC came with a copy of Windows XP already installed, the sticker with the product key may be on the PC itself or on a separate slip of paper.

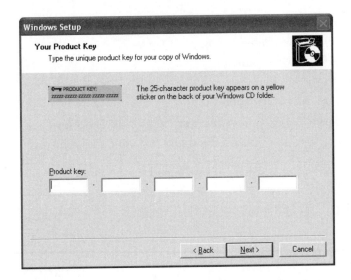

Figure 2   *To reinstall or repair Windows XP, you must enter the unique 25-character product key in this space.*

Do not lose the product key or the CD! If you do, you're setting yourself up for heartache sometime in the future. Without a valid product key, you'll be unable to reinstall or repair Windows. Each product key is unique, and when you install Windows you have to *activate* your copy with Microsoft. You can use your product key to reinstall Windows on the same computer where it was originally activated, but if you try to reuse a product key that's already been used on a different computer, you'll be unable to activate it.

TIP   If you've misplaced the sticker with your product key, don't despair. As long as your current copy of Windows XP is installed and working properly, you can recover the key. Download a free utility called Keyfinder from Magical Jelly Bean Software at *http://www.magicaljellybean.com/ keyfinder.shtml*. Unzip the program file and run it. Keyfinder extracts the product key from your saved settings; print out the key, and keep it with your Windows CD. (If you use Microsoft Office, this program also collects your Office product keys.)

☐ Gather your program disks

How many programs do you have installed on your old PC? Ten? Twenty? Too many to count? I have some bad news for you: there is no easy way to move those programs to your new PC. Although you can transfer all of your saved documents and some of your program settings without too much effort, you'll need to reinstall each one of those programs.

Start by making a list of all the programs installed on your old computer that you want to transfer to your new PC. From Control Panel, open **Add or Remove Programs** to see the list of everything that Windows knows about. You might also want to click

NOTE The silver lining? Your old computer is probably cluttered with programs you no longer use. When you set up your new PC, you can ditch all those old programs and get a fresh start.

Start and then click **Programs** (for older Windows versions) or **All Programs** (for Windows XP). The list of program shortcuts on this menu should jog your memory.

When the time comes to reinstall your software, you'll need the original program CDs for those programs you didn't acquire by downloading, along with any serial numbers, product keys, or specialized installation instructions for those programs. At a minimum, I strongly recommend that you do this *now* for any programs that fall into either of the following categories:

- **Programs you use every day.** If you use Microsoft Word or PowerPoint in your daily work, you'd better make sure you have your Microsoft Office CD close at hand!

- **Programs required by specific hardware devices.** My wife uses a handheld Palm computer, and I use a Pocket PC. Both devices require synchronization software that isn't included with a new computer. Needless to say, I keep those CDs in a safe place.

☐ Collect your downloaded programs

These days, not all programs come on CDs. In fact, an increasing number are delivered electronically. Out of 50 programs installed on the computer I'm using right now, 42 were downloaded and only eight are on CDs. If your software collection is anything like mine, you have dozens of downloaded programs on your hard disk. When you set up your new PC, you'll waste a lot of time if you have to download all those programs again, and you'll waste even more time if you have to search for serial numbers and installation instructions to get them working.

If you're like most people, you store downloaded programs in a variety of locations—on the desktop, in the My Documents folder, or wherever the Save As dialog box happens to be pointing when you download a file. I recommend that you look for these downloaded program files on your hard disk and pull all of them together into one well-organized Downloads folder. You can then transfer the whole collection to your new PC by copying that folder, and when you're ready to reinstall that software, you can do so quickly and efficiently by working through all the items stored there. Spending a few extra minutes getting organized now will save you hours of time later.

Find the list of programs on your old PC that you want to reinstall on your new PC. (You created this list during the previous step, "Gather your program disks.") For each of those programs that you acquired by downloading, your goal is to find the original program files and organize them in a common location. (The files themselves might be compressed Zip files, executable programs, or Windows Installer files.) If you can't find the files for a favorite program, or if your downloaded copy is more than a year old, find the software maker's Web site and download a fresh copy. (A program's Help menu often includes the software maker's Web address; if not, use your favorite search engine to track it down.)

Finally, go through your old e-mail, printed receipts, and other sources to find serial numbers, product keys, and other important information you might need to reinstall the software. This information is especially important when you've downloaded a trial version of a program and then paid to upgrade it to the registered version. You'll need to supply your proof of purchase when you install the program on your new PC to unlock its full set of features.

Here's how you can mirror the system I use to keep downloads organized:

1   In the My Documents folder, create a subfolder called Downloads.

2   Within the Downloads folder, create a subfolder for each downloaded program you'll want on your new PC. If you've downloaded the popular WinZip program, for instance, create a folder called WinZip.

3   Download the programs on your list that you're replacing with freshly updated copies. Now place the file or files for each downloaded program on your list into its related subfolder. Create a shortcut to the Web site from which you downloaded the program and place it in this subfolder as well, along with any notes about installing or registering the program. If a serial number or product key is required for installation, save that information in a text file along with the program files in the subfolder.

Every few months, I go through the Downloads folder and click the Web shortcut for each program I use regularly to see if a newer version is available. If I find an upgrade, I replace the existing file with the new one and upgrade the currently installed version. Then, I burn the contents of my Downloads folder to a CD or DVD, label it with the current date, and store it with the rest of my disks and documents.

Getting organized this way takes some extra time initially, but once your Downloads folder is created, it takes only a few extra seconds to create a new subfolder to store a new downloaded program. And you'll save plenty of time if you ever need to reinstall a program.

☐ Print out your Internet and e-mail settings

In the 21st century, a computer without an Internet connection might as well be a paperweight. Transferring your Internet settings to your new PC can be a tricky process. You can increase the odds of success by gathering your most important settings before you make the switch.

- Do you have a broadband connection, such as a cable modem or DSL line? If so, you'll want to contact your Internet service provider (ISP). You probably won't require a user name or password, but some ISPs (especially cable companies) tie your connection to a unique identifier on your network card, called a MAC address. If you switch to a new computer with a new network card, your ISP may need to reset your connection using the new MAC address.

- Do you use a dial-up connection through a local or national ISP? Make sure you know your user name, password, and local access number. The Windows XP Files and Settings Transfer Wizard (which we'll get to on page 108) will transfer all the details of your connection except your password. If you can't remember your password, call your ISP and ask them to assign you a new one.

- Are you an AOL or MSN subscriber? For best results, get the latest access software. Over a dial-up connection, the download can take hours. If you don't have a CD handy, call and ask to have one mailed to you.

And don't forget to write down the details of your e-mail accounts. You'll need your user name (usually the same as your e-mail address) and your password—note that this user name/password combination might be different from the one you use to connect to the Internet. For Internet-standard e-mail accounts (not AOL or MSN), you'll also need the names of your incoming (POP3) and outgoing (SMTP) mail servers. If you currently use Outlook Express, you can find this information without too much effort:

1 Open Outlook Express, click **Tools**, and then click **Accounts**.

2 Click the Mail tab, and click to select the account whose details you want to inspect.

3 Click **Properties**.

4 Print out or write down the information on the **Servers** tab, as shown in Figure 3.

Figure 3 *Make a note of e-mail account information, especially the names of incoming and out-going mail servers.*

If other people share your computer, make sure you write down their e-mail settings, too.

Do you have more than one e-mail account? If you have a Web-based e-mail account, such as Hotmail, or a secondary account for work, be sure to record its details as well.

TIP   Normally, your e-mail password is saved on your computer, but for security purposes it's displayed as a row of asterisks. If you can't find the password in your records, you can use a free utility to find the text hidden behind the asterisks. Download the Revelation utility from *www.snadboy.com* and install it. Follow the program's instructions to reveal the hidden passwords—and this time, write them down!

☐ Make a note of your network settings

If you plan to connect your new PC to a local area network (often referred to as a "LAN") in a home or small business, Windows XP does most of the setup work automatically. You may need to adjust settings manually if your network contains any of the following elements:

- **A broadband router.** At a minimum, you'll need to know how to access the configuration page for the router. You'll find these details in the router's manual.

- **A connection to a corporate network.** If you use your home PC to work with your corporate network, you may need to set up a Virtual Private Network (VPN) or install remote access software. Your corporate support staff should be able to provide you with step-by-step instructions.

- **Manually configured network devices.** These days, it's rare for a computer to use manual network configurations. Most computers running Windows XP can get an IP address, subnet mask, and other settings automatically. If you have a network printer or other specialized device, however, you may need to enter its configuration details manually.

- **Wireless devices.** Once a curiosity, wireless networking is rapidly becoming the preferred way to connect computers, printers, handheld devices, and home entertainment systems in one big network. If your new PC includes a wireless (Wi-Fi) network card, you'll need to make sure you know how to get connected to your wireless access point. Windows XP includes drivers and configuration tools for Wi-Fi equipment; you'll need to know the name of the access point (also called the SSID) and its encryption key.

The Short Version

You're busy. You want to get started with your new PC *right now*, and you certainly don't want to read this book cover to cover first.

I understand. Really, I do. I feel exactly the same way sometimes. Patience may be a virtue, but impatience is human nature. That's why I wrote this chapter and put it at the front of the book. The steps I've listed here are the absolutely essential ones that you can't afford to skip. If you don't have the time or the patience to go through this entire book right now, make sure you do everything I describe in this chapter. You'll thank me later.

This chapter serves another important function—even if you plan to go through the book in order, step by step, you can get a solid overview of what I recommend for your new PC by quickly reviewing the material here first. That way you'll have an idea of what to expect at every step.

A word of caution first: in this chapter I assume that you understand the mechanics of each of these tasks, and I don't include a lot of details. If you're a bit rusty on some Microsoft Windows procedures, look up the corresponding chapter later in this book to see the full instructions.

Ready? OK, let's get started.

Hook up all the pieces

If you have a garden-variety desktop PC, you'll start with the CPU, which is typically a tower that contains the processor, memory, disk drives, and ports for connecting external devices. Plug the CPU and your monitor into an AC power source, and then connect the keyboard, mouse, monitor, and speakers to their respective ports on the back of the CPU. Don't connect your modem to the phone line or your network card to a cable modem yet, and ignore any other external devices you might have, such as digital cameras and scanners. (We'll get to them in a few minutes.)

If you have a notebook computer, the job is much simpler. Make sure your battery is inserted in the notebook, and then connect the external power supply to an AC power source. If your portable PC has an external CD or DVD drive, connect it now. Turn on the computer and leave it connected to AC power during all setup activities.

TIP   If you're comfortable with technical settings, this is a good time to learn how to access your computer's BIOS—the place where your PC stores detailed configuration information. If you're lucky, the boot screen includes a reminder of exactly which key to press to get into the BIOS; if not, you'll need to look it up in the computer's manual. Look through the BIOS to ensure that your memory, hard disks, and other devices are installed correctly.

Answer a few questions

If you've purchased a new, name-brand computer, you'll need to run through what's called the "out of the box" setup process the first time you turn it on. You can't skip this step, but you can go through it quickly. Most of the prompts are self-explanatory: you'll be asked to accept a license agreement, enter your name and your company name, and give your computer a name. Keep it short, and don't give your computer the same name you plan to use to log on.

During this phase of the setup process, Windows asks you if you want to set up Internet access. Just say no—we'll do that in a few minutes. But do set up a user account when prompted to do so. If you skip this option, Windows sets up a default account called Administrator (in Windows XP Professional) or Owner (Windows XP Home Edition).

After you complete this guided setup, restart your computer. When you reach the Welcome screen, click your user account name to log on to Windows and get to the Windows desktop.

Install Service Pack 2, if necessary

Do you have the latest updates for Windows XP on your new PC? Specifically, is Service Pack 2 (SP2) installed? This isn't just a techno-trivia question; the improvements in SP2 include some sweeping changes to security features that can help protect you from viruses, worms, spyware, and other Internet-based threats.

If you buy a shiny new PC with Windows XP preinstalled, it probably already includes SP2. If you built your own PC, if you upgraded a PC by using a Windows XP CD you bought in 2004 or earlier, or if your PC maker was a bit behind the technological curve, you might be using an older version.

NOTE Service Pack 2 is an incredibly important update to Windows XP. Throughout this book, I assume that you've installed SP2. If you haven't, some of my advice will make no sense. More importantly, your computer will be exposed to unacceptable security risks. Please don't put it off. If you haven't yet installed SP2, do it now!

To see whether SP2 is installed, click **Start**, point to My Computer and right-click, and then click **Properties**. On the General tab, look at the text below the **System:** heading. If you see the words **Service Pack 2** here, as shown in Figure 1, you can skip to the next step and set up your Internet connection. If you don't see these magic words, your first priority should be to bring your computer up to date by installing SP2.

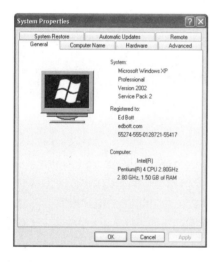

Figure 1   *This dialog box lets you see at a glance whether Service Pack 2 is installed.*

The ideal way to install SP2 on a new PC is to use an "official" CD from Microsoft. A close second choice, if you have access to another PC with a fast Internet connection and a CD burner, is to download the full service pack—you can find the link at *http://www.microsoft.com/security*—and burn your own CD. If you don't have either kind of CD handy, you'll need to download the service pack—carefully—after you connect to the Internet.

Set up your Internet connection

As the Blaster worm proved several years ago, destructive computer viruses can jump onto your computer over an unprotected Internet connection. In fact, many frustrated Blaster victims discovered the Catch-22 of computer security: you need to download Critical Updates to protect yourself from viruses and worms, but you have to connect to the Internet to download those updates. How do you avoid being victimized by worms and hackers when you first update your computer?

Your first layer of defense is to turn on the built-in firewall in Windows XP and enable a baseline level of security. If Service Pack 2 is **CAUTION** Don't plug in your network cable or modem yet.
already installed on your computer, the Windows Firewall is automatically enabled and you can skip the rest of this paragraph. If you use a dial-up Internet connection and your computer has no network card, you can also skip past the rest of this paragraph as well. If you have a broadband (cable modem or DSL) network and you're using the original release of Windows XP (with or without Service Pack 1), open Control Panel, click **Network and Internet Connections**, and then click **Network Connections**. Right-click the Local Area Connection icon and click **Properties**. On the Advanced tab, click to select the **Internet Connection Firewall** check box. Click **OK** to close this dialog box, but leave the Network Connections folder open.

Now that you've enabled the firewall, you can plug in your network card (or connect your modem to the phone line) and set up your Internet connection. If you have other computers that you want to add to your local area network, you can plug them into the network hub or router and set up your network at the same time. (For full details on broadband connections, see "Set up a high-speed Internet connection," beginning on page 59. For more details about setting up a network, with or without a broadband Internet connection, see "Step 3: Get Connected," beginning on page 84.)

If you have a dial-up Internet connection, a wizard sets it up for you. Click **Start**, click **Control Panel**, and click **Network and Internet Connections**. Under the **Pick a task...** heading, click **Set up or change your Internet connection**. This opens the Internet Properties dialog box and displays the Connections tab. Click **Setup** to start the New Connection Wizard. Click **Next** to move each of the wizard's screens, following the prompts to set up your connection. On the **Network Connection Type** page, choose **Connect to the Internet**. On the **Getting Ready** page, choose **Set up my connection manually**. You'll need to give your connection a descriptive name, supply the local access phone number, and enter your login name and password. When you finish, save the new connection and move to "Install additional Critical Updates" on page 18.

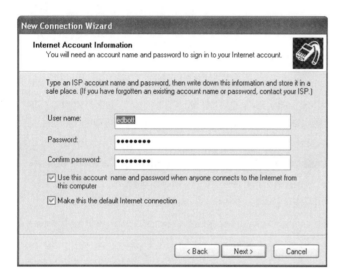

If you have a broadband connection, it should work without any extra configuration effort on your part. Use the Network Setup Wizard to make sure the Windows Firewall is set up properly. On the left side of the Network Connections folder, under the heading **Network Tasks**, click **Set up a home or small office network**. (Don't get confused—this is the correct way to set up an Internet connection as well, even if you have no network and yours is the only computer around for miles.) In the Network Setup Wizard, follow the prompts; the text does a good job of explaining your options.

If you have a local area network, the SP2 version of the Network Setup Wizard asks if you want to enable file sharing. Choose whichever option you prefer. If you change your mind, you can always run the wizard again.

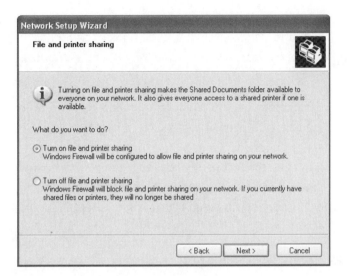

When you finish, the wizard runs through a series of configuration steps and you're ready to access the Internet. The final step allows you to create a Network Setup disk you can use to set up other computers on your local network. Go ahead and create the disk if you want to—you can also use the Windows XP CD—but don't set up the rest of your networked computers until you've finished updating your computer.

I know you're tempted to browse to a few Web pages or check your e-mail, but don't do it yet! We still need to take care of some essential security steps.

> **TIP** If you're not sure which options to choose in the Network Setup Wizard, just use the default settings and click Next when prompted. You can always re-run the wizard later if you need to adjust any settings.

 # Install additional Critical Updates

Now that you've got a working Internet connection, the very first task you should complete is to finish Windows Update and install all available Critical Updates. You'll find shortcuts to Windows Update just about everywhere in Windows. I prefer to click **Start**, click **All Programs**, and click the Windows Update icon at the top of the All Programs menu.

If this is the first time you've visited Windows Update, you'll probably need to download a program that installs the Windows Update code on your computer. Click **Yes** in the security dialog box that asks whether it's OK to install the Windows Update control.

When you reach the Windows Update page, the Windows Update control will scan your computer to see which updates you need. After the scan is complete, choose the option that includes Critical Updates and Service Packs. If you haven't yet installed Service Pack 2, this should be the first item in the list. (Figure 2 shows what you might see on Windows Update.) You need to install SP2 separately. Depending on the speed of your Internet connection, this could take a few minutes or it could take hours.

Figure 2   *If Service Pack 2 is available via Windows Update, install it before downloading any other updates.*

After you complete the installation of SP2 and restart your computer, you'll be asked to set up Automatic Updates. When you return to the Windows desktop, run Windows Update again and install all other Critical Updates. If you want to set up your local network by using the Network Setup disk you created previously, now's the time.

NOTE Service Packs are cumulative, meaning that everything in Service Pack 1 is included in Service Pack 2. If you're updating a copy of the original release of Windows XP, just install SP2, not SP1 and then SP2.

Check your security settings

Windows XP Service Pack 2 includes a new utility called the Windows Security Center. Its job is to monitor three crucial security settings to ensure that you're not vulnerable to security risks. This component isn't optional, and it can't be removed. To check your Security Center settings, click **Start**, click **Control Panel**, and double-click **Security Center**. If the three items under **Security essentials** show a green ON icon, you're in good shape. If any of them are yellow or red, you need to check the settings and make any necessary adjustments. The following three sections discuss each of these items in more detail. (For the complete picture, read "Step 2: Protect Your PC," beginning on page 56.)

TIP   I strongly recommend that you pay careful attention to any warnings that you see in the Security Center. The Help text offers excellent explanations of each feature, and an assortment of buttons make it easy to enable, disable, or configure any of these features.

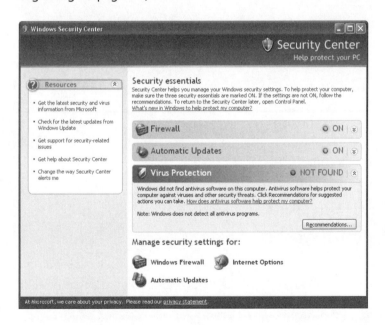

Configure the Windows Firewall

The original release of Windows XP included a security feature called the Internet Connection Firewall (ICF). It offered effective protection against outside attackers and worms that can spread over networks (including the Internet). Unfortunately, it caused problems with some programs and networks, and it was disabled by default. Most Windows XP users never knew this firewall even existed. SP2 replaces the old ICF with an all-new program called the Windows Firewall. It's turned on by default, and it works well with other programs and networks. To check its settings, open Security Center and click the Windows Firewall icon at the bottom of the dialog box. Figure 3 shows the firewall settings.

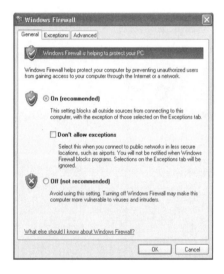

Figure 3   *Turn off the Windows Firewall only if you have a replacement for it.*

Most people will choose to leave the Windows Firewall on, using its default settings. You should make some adjustments only if the following conditions apply:

- **You've installed a third-party firewall program.** Full-featured security packages often include a firewall component that adds bells and whistles not included in the bare-bones Windows Firewall. If you have a separate firewall program, you don't need the Windows Firewall and you can safely click **Off (not recommended)** here.

- **You have one or more programs that are blocked by the firewall's default settings.** Windows will automatically configure most programs to work correctly through the firewall. In some rare cases, you might find that a favorite online game or file-transfer program doesn't behave properly and you might need to tweak the Windows Firewall configuration. Click the Exceptions tab to add a new program or port to this list. The software documentation should provide the details you need for this step.

Set up Automatic Updates

As I noted earlier in this chapter, Critical Updates are your first line of defense against Trojan horse programs and spyware. By default, Windows XP checks Microsoft's update servers regularly and downloads these patches as they become available. If you enabled the Automatic Updates option when you installed SP2 (or when you ran through the "out of the box" setup), these updates are automatically installed in the middle of the night (at 3:00 AM, to be precise). After installing the update, Windows restarts your computer if necessary.

This option is the safest way to ensure that you never miss an important update. However, you risk losing data if you leave a document open and unsaved at the end of the day and your computer automatically restarts itself to apply an update.

I prefer to adjust this setting so that Windows automatically downloads the updates for me and notifies me that they're ready to be installed. To set this option, open Security Center and click the Automatic Updates icon. In the Automatic Updates dialog box, click **Download updates for me, but let me choose when to install them**.

CAUTION If you change the Automatic Updates option as I just described, Windows will notify you when new updates are ready to be installed. It's human nature to close these notifications and postpone installing the update, because this task tends to interfere with daily work or play. When you see an update notification, pay attention to it. Usually, installation takes only a few minutes; don't postpone the update any longer than you have to.

After you make this change, the Automatic Updates entry in Windows Security Center will no longer display a green icon; instead, it displays a yellow **Check Settings** label. Don't be alarmed.

❑ Add antivirus software and update it

SP2 includes a slew of new security features, but one feature on prominent display in the Windows Security Center isn't included with the operating system. I can't imagine operating a computer without effective, up-to-date antivirus software, and neither should you. For effective protection, you need more than just the software package; you also need to configure the program so that it updates itself automatically. Without the latest updates, you're vulnerable to every new virus.

If your new PC included a trial subscription to an antivirus package, give it a try. If you like it, renew the subscription for a full year. If you prefer an alternative, now's the time to install it. After installing the software, run its update option to install the latest antivirus signatures and program

NOTE For recommendations on how to find the right antivirus software, see "Install antivirus software," on page 71. This section also includes more detailed instructions on how to configure several popular antivirus programs.

code. Then, run the update program again; ironically, some updates turn out to have updates of their own. Finally, follow the program's instructions to configure automatic updates.

❑ Transfer files from your old computer

When setting up your new PC, this is the biggest hassle you're likely to face. Even if you've done this before, it's easy to leave behind an important file or two. And unfortunately, none of the options move your programs from your old PC to the new one. You have two options:

● **Transfer your files manually.** If you don't have that many data files, you can use a Zip drive or a network connection to copy just the files you need. Don't forget to copy your e-mail. If you created a Downloads folder to organize your downloaded programs, as I recommended on page 9, be sure to copy this folder as well.

- **Use the Windows XP Files and Settings Transfer Wizard.** This utility does an excellent job of transferring your Windows preferences, some program settings, and all your data files to your new PC. You can use a network connection, which is by far the easiest method and the one I recommend. If you find it impractical to set up a network, use an external hard drive or a direct cable connection.

After setting up your network connection, start the wizard on the new computer first, by clicking **Start**, then **All Programs**, then **Accessories**, then **System Tools**, and finally **Files and Settings Transfer Wizard**. Follow the wizard's prompts, specifying that this is the new computer. On the **Do you have a Windows XP CD?** page, click **I will use the wizard from the Windows XP CD**. Click Next, and you'll find yourself at the dialog box shown here:

NOTE Getting the Files and Settings Transfer Wizard to work properly can be tricky, even if you've used it before. In this brief explanation, I assume you've connected the two computers in a network. If you've chosen a different option, read the fuller explanation that begins on page 117 in "Step 4: Move Files and Settings." In fact, even if you're a certified Windows expert, I highly recommend that you read that chapter in full to get the most out of this utility.

Files and Settings Transfer Wizard

Now go to your old computer.

To collect your files and settings:

1. Go to your old computer and insert the Windows XP CD into the CD-ROM drive.
2. On the CD menu that appears, click Perform additional tasks.
3. On the next menu that appears, click Transfer files and settings.

Note: If a menu does not appear, click Start, and then click Run. Type D:\setup where D: is your CD-ROM drive, and then click OK.

After you collect your files and settings from your old computer, return here, and then click Next.

Or, if you are using the direct cable method to transfer files and settings, click Next to go to the following page, and select Direct cable.

[< Back]   [Next >]   [Cancel]

Now insert the Windows XP CD in the old computer's CD-ROM drive. From the **What do you want to do?** menu, click **Perform additional tasks**, and then click **Transfer files and settings**. Follow the wizard's prompts, specifying that this is the old computer and choosing **Home or small office network** as the transfer option. You can customize which files and settings you want to transfer, using the options shown in Figure 4. Click **Next** to begin the transfer.

TIP   I recommend that you wait at least a week before erasing the data files on your old computer. The Files and Settings Transfer Wizard works well, but it's far from foolproof, and it may take several days before you realize that one or more important files are missing.

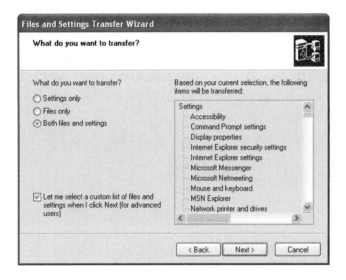

Figure 4   *Click the check box in the lower left corner of this dialog box to specify exactly which files and settings get migrated to your new computer.*

Set up your e-mail

If you've been using Outlook Express or Microsoft Outlook on your old computer, the Files and Settings Transfer Wizard should have automatically migrated your e-mail account settings, all of your messages, and your address book. (You'll need to enter the passwords for each transferred account.) If you didn't use the wizard and you don't care about your old messages, you can set up your e-mail accounts from

TIP   Have you forgotten your e-mail password? See the Tip on page 12 for a suggestion on how you might be able to read the hidden, saved password from your old PC.

scratch. (As I explained in the "Before You Begin" chapter, you'll need your account details—specifically user name, password, and the names of incoming and outgoing servers.)

The following procedure works with Outlook Express. If you use a different e-mail program, you'll need to enter the same data using the procedures that are appropriate for that program.

1 Open Outlook Express. Click **Tools**, and then click **Accounts**.

2 In the Accounts dialog box, click **Add**. Click **Mail** from the shortcut menu.

3 Follow the wizard's prompts to enter the following information:

- Your display name, which appears in the From field of any message you send.

- Your e-mail address.

- Your account type: choose **POP3** for most dial-up accounts, or **HTTP** if you're setting up an MSN or Hotmail account. (The **IMAP** option is an advanced configuration that you're unlikely to run into.)

> **NOTE** Do you use AOL for e-mail? Then you'll need to set up your AOL software to collect your messages. Outlook Express does not support AOL mail, nor do most other third-party e-mail programs.

- For POP3 accounts, the names of incoming and outgoing e-mail servers.

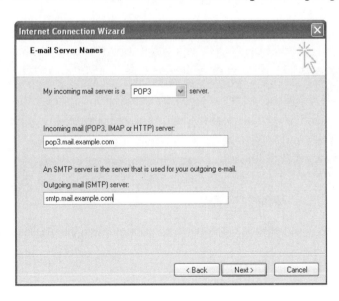

- Your account name.

- Your password, if you want it to be saved with your account information. Leave this field blank if you want to be prompted for your password every time you open Outlook Express and check your e-mail through this account.

If you have additional e-mail accounts, set them up now as well.

Set up your printer and other hardware

The one hardware device nearly everyone has is a printer. If your printer is relatively new, Windows XP probably includes the hardware drivers it needs. If the printer uses a USB connection and you're certain it's fully compatible with Windows XP, plug it in now and let Windows Plug and Play do its magic. After a flurry of status messages, you should have a working printer in a matter of minutes.

If your printer is more than a year old—or if it's a multifunction machine that scans and faxes, too—you'll probably need to install some supporting files first. Look for the CD that came with the printer. After verifying that the software on the CD is intended for Windows XP, go ahead and run the Setup program from the CD.

TIP   With printers in particular, I recommend that you always check for newer drivers before installing. Visit the Support section of the printer manufacturer's Web site, and search for downloads related to the model number of your printer or multifunction device.

If you have an older printer that uses a parallel connection instead of a USB port, follow these steps to install the printer:

1 One end of the parallel cable should already be connected to your printer. With the printer powered off, plug the connector at the other end of the cable into your PC's parallel port.

2 Turn the printer's power on.

3 Click **Start,** and then click **Printers and Faxes**.

4 In the Printers and Faxes folder, under the **Printer Tasks** heading on the left, click **Add a printer**.

5   Follow the wizard's prompts. When you reach the dialog box shown here, select the **Automatically detect and install my Plug and Play printer** check box:

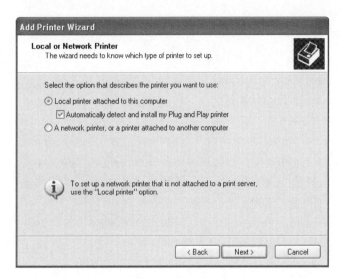

6   Supply a driver disk, if necessary, and complete the remaining steps of the wizard to install the correct driver.

If you have any external hardware devices, such as a digital camera or scanner, set them up now as well. For USB-based devices, the rules are simple: install the drivers first (either from the CD included with the device or from a downloaded file), plug in the device, and let the Windows Plug and Play feature tackle the rest of the work. Verify that each device works before moving on. (You'll find much more specific advice in "Step 5: Set Up Printers, Digital Cameras, and Other Hardware," which begins on page 128.)

Install your favorite software programs

If you followed my recommendations in "Before You Begin," this job might be a little boring, but it shouldn't be complicated. Start with the stack of program CDs you assembled, and install each one in turn. In most cases, a Setup program will run automatically when you pop the CD into your CD-ROM drive. If nothing happens, search the CD for the correct setup files and double-click the listing in Windows Explorer.

Next, open Windows Explorer and browse to the Downloads folder you created to organize your downloaded program files. Go through each subfolder and install the program from the files stored there. After installing each one, be sure to start the program and confirm that it works as you intended. Open and create new data files, if appropriate, and also make sure you can find all the data files you transferred from your old PC (earlier in this chapter, during the "Transfer files from your old computer" step).

TIP   If you are installing any version of Microsoft Office, you'll need to start by installing the Office programs from the CD. After completing the installation, visit the Office Online Web site (*http://office.microsoft.com*) and click Check for Updates. As with Windows Update, you'll first need to install a small program that scans your PC to check for required updates; from the resulting list, install the latest service packs and patches.

Personalize your new PC

If you ran the Files and Settings Transfer Wizard previously, some of these settings have already been changed from their default values to match the ones on your old PC. This is a good time to review any or all of the groups of settings listed below. (A more complete version of this list appears in "Step 7: Personalize and Organize"; the list begins on page 172.) With a bit of tweaking now, you can get your new PC working in sync with your preferences. In the following list, I describe where to find each group of settings and I list examples of changes I typically make to a new PC:

- **Control Panel.** Click **Start**, and then click **Control Panel**. I prefer to see these icons stored in a single alphabetical list rather than organized in categories, so I click **Switch to Classic View** under the **Control Panel** heading in the tasks pane on the left.

- **Display properties.** Right-click any empty space on the Windows desktop, and click **Properties**. Use the **Screen resolution** slider and the **Color quality** list on the Settings tab to change the dimensions of your screen; a lower resolution is easier to read, and a higher one lets you see more information. On the Desktop tab, choose a favorite picture to use as your background. Click the Screen Saver tab to configure a screen saver. On my work PC, I click **On resume, display Welcome screen**, to prevent nosy co-workers from peeking at what I'm working on when I step away.

- **Internet Explorer security and privacy settings.** Open Internet Explorer, click **Tools**, and then click **Internet Options**. On the Security tab, you can tighten security for various types of Web sites—this tab is for expert use. On the Privacy tab, make sure **Block pop-ups** is selected and then click **Settings** to fine-tune which pop-up windows get blocked and which are allowed to pass. (This feature is new in SP2.)

- **Internet Explorer advanced settings.** On the Advanced tab of the Internet Options dialog box, you'll find a long list of mostly esoteric settings. A few are genuinely useful, though, such as the ones under the **Search from the Address bar** heading.

- **Windows Messenger/MSN Messenger.** If you use either of these popular chat programs, enable them to log on using your Passport automatically. If you don't want Windows Messenger to start automatically, click **Start**, click **All Programs**, and then click **Windows Messenger**. From the Messenger window, click **Tools**, and then click **Options**. On the Preferences tab, clear the top two options, **Run Windows Messenger when Windows starts** and **Allow Windows Messenger to run in the background**. (You'll need to clear a matching option in Outlook Express. Click **Tools**, click **Options**, and then clear **Automatically log on to Windows Messenger** on the General tab. Finally, in Outlook Express, click **View**, then **Layout**, and clear the **Contacts** check box.)

- **Mouse and keyboard.** The Mouse option and the Keyboard option in Control Panel allow you to adjust the sensitivity of these input devices. I use a wheel mouse and routinely adjust the settings on the Wheel tab so that each click of the wheel scrolls six lines instead of three in Internet Explorer and Outlook Express.

- **Date and time.** Double-click the clock at the right side of the taskbar. (This is quicker than opening the Date and Time icon from Control Panel.) Adjust the time and date, if necessary, and then click the Internet Time tab to ensure that Windows automatically updates the time from authoritative servers on the Internet.

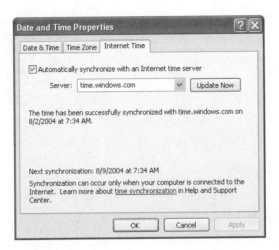

● **Sounds.** From the Sounds and Audio Devices option in Control Panel, you can make a variety of settings to the way your system handles sound. On the Volume tab, click the **Place volume icon in the taskbar** option to give yourself quicker access to a volume control and mute button. On the Sounds tab, you can choose predefined collections of sounds or change the sounds associated with a single event.

- **Taskbar and Start menu.** Right-click the **Start** button and click **Properties** to open a dialog box that gives you access to dozens of interesting settings. On the Taskbar tab, you can lock the taskbar (so that you don't accidentally make it too small or too wide or move it to the side of the screen). On the Start Menu tab, you can replace the Windows XP–style Start menu with the Classic Start menu (the style used in Windows 98). Click **Customize** to change options associated with the style of Start menu you've chosen.

- **Fonts.** The Fonts folder, available from Control Panel, shows all installed fonts on your PC. To add a font to your system, drag it into this folder.

- **Recycle Bin.** Right-click the Recycle Bin icon on the desktop, and click **Properties**. By default, Windows asks you to confirm your action each time you delete a file. I find those dialog boxes annoying, so I make sure to clear this !

- **Windows Explorer settings.** From Control Panel, double-click **Folder Options**. You're most likely to want to change options on the View tab, shown here. For instance, you can decide whether to show or hide system files, whether to show the Address bar, and whether you want to reopen all the folder windows you were previously working with each time you start Windows.

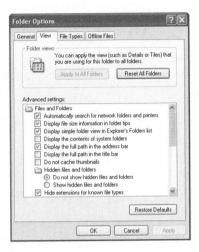

Clean up your old PC

What are you planning to do with your old computer? Give it away to a friend or relative? Let the kids use it for games and homework? Throw it away? Before you hand over the computer to someone else, make sure you wipe away any sensitive or personal information. The easiest solution is to reformat the hard disk, reinstall the original operating system, and update. In the final chapter of this book, "Clean Up Your Old Computer," which begins on page 202, I explain how to find tools that can wipe files from the hard disk so that they can't be recovered easily and how to safely and responsibly recycle old computer parts instead of simply dumping them in the nearest landfill.

Step 1: **Out of the Box**

Whether your new PC is a traditional desktop design or a notebook, some assembly is required. Most new PCs come with a "quick setup" guide, in the form of a poster or a small, illustrated booklet, the purpose of which is to show you how to put together the pieces of your new PC. If your computer came with one of these guides, by all means follow its instructions.

The "out of box experience" isn't limited to hardware. When you first turn on a new PC with Microsoft Windows XP preinstalled, you typically step through an introductory sequence designed to help you perform some simple setup tasks. You can't avoid this process, but don't expect it to accomplish any more than the absolute essentials. The most important part of this process is to create a user account for yourself. Don't worry about creating accounts for other people in your family at this point. You'll have a chance to do that later.

Finally, the manufacturer of your computer may have added some custom setup steps for you to complete the first time you turn on your new PC. These steps might involve configuring additional software that the PC maker installed on your computer or providing you with an opportunity to sign up for online services such as Internet access or online banking.

After you complete these initial setup steps, you can move on to the rest of this chapter, in which I show you how to make sure all the pieces of your new PC— hardware and software—are working right.

☑ Checklist:

☐ **Hook up the hardware (page 38).** Connect the CPU and monitor to AC power, plug in the keyboard, mouse, monitor, and speakers, and turn everything on. Don't worry about other devices for now, and don't connect to the Internet yet.

☐ **Run through Windows Setup (page 40).** If this is the first time you've turned on your new PC, Windows XP has a few questions for you.

☐ **Take inventory: hardware (page 42).** Get out your invoice and make sure you have the memory, hard disk, and other devices you paid for. Also, check to see that drives (floppy, CD, DVD) work properly and that your system fan is working.

☐ **Take inventory: software (page 45).** Make sure you have the correct version of Windows installed (you can find details on the System Properties dialog box), and make sure you store your 25-character product key in a safe place.

☐ **Check your hard disk format (page 46).** Open the My Computer window, right-click the icon for your main hard disk in the **Hard Disk Drives** category, and then click **Properties**. Verify that the drive is formatted using the NTFS file system. If the drive is formatted as FAT32, use the Convert utility to change the file system.

☐ **Set up a user account for each person who uses your PC (page 48).** If you share your computer with kids or co-workers, consider giving them Limited accounts. Users you trust can be designated as Administrators.

☐ **Add a password to your user account (page 50).** This is an important security precaution, even if you don't share your computer with other people or use it on a network. Your password should be one that you can easily remember but that won't be easily guessed by someone who knows you.

☐ **Create a password reset disk (page 52).** You'll find this option in Control Panel, under the User Accounts section. You can save the encrypted password to a floppy disk or a USB flash memory drive. Store it in a safe place.

☐ **Test and troubleshoot (page 54).** Before you spend a lot of time setting up your computer, make sure everything works properly. If you run into problems, check this section for some troubleshooting advice.

Hook up the hardware

If your new PC is a standard desktop model, it consists of at least four pieces: a central processing unit, or CPU, which is the box that contains the computer's guts; a monitor; a keyboard; and a mouse. You probably also have a pair of external speakers, which you'll connect as part of this step, and you may have some other devices, which you should ignore for now (because we'll get to them later).

The front of the CPU usually includes a power button, various status lights, and access to removable drives where you can insert a CD or DVD. You might also see some ports designed to let you plug in removable devices, such as a digital camera or a portable music player. Don't worry about these devices right now. Instead, turn the CPU around and look at the back, where you should see a collection of ports that looks something like Figure 1.

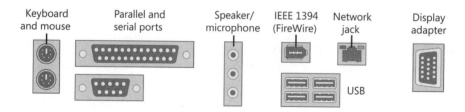

Figure 1   *The back of your PC should have most of these ports, although they may be arranged differently.*

Here's what you need to do:

1 **Connect the keyboard and mouse.** If the plug at the end of the cord issuing from either device has a round connector, plug it into the matching port on the back of the computer, like the one shown at left on the next page. If you find a flat connector at the end of the cord, plug it into any available USB port, like the one shown at right on the next page. (Most computers have between two and six USB ports, which can be used to connect all sorts of external

TIP   Many PCs use color-coded combinations of connectors and ports that take the guesswork out of making sure each plug goes in the right place. On several of my computers with motherboards made by Intel Corporation, for instance, the mouse connector is green and the keyboard connector is purple. If I'm crawling around under my desk, I don't have to guess which is which: I just plug the green connector into the green port and the purple connector into the purple port.

devices to expand your computer's capabilities.) Both types of connectors are designed so that you can't plug the connector in the wrong way.

2 **Attach the monitor to the display adapter.** Most monitors use a standard analog cable with a 15-pin connector that plugs into a matching port on the back of the PC. (A well-labeled PC will include a monitor icon next to this port.) Some specialized monitors use digital connectors, which require a matching digital display adapter and a custom cable.

3 **Connect your speakers to the computer's audio output.** The connector for stereo speakers is typically color-coded lime green. If you have a fancy surround sound system, check the computer manual to see where to plug in the center and back speakers. If the speaker cables and the sound card use connectors and ports that don't match, you may need to visit an electronics or audio specialty store to buy an adapter cable.

4 **Connect the CPU to an AC power source.** Look for the thick power cord, usually black or beige, that came with your computer. Plug the female end into the power supply on the back of the computer, and plug the male end into a wall socket. If you have a surge protector or an uninterruptible power supply connected to your AC power, plug the CPU into that power source instead.

5   **Connect the monitor to an AC power source.** Then press the power switch on the monitor to turn it on.

6   **Push the power switch on the front of the PC.**

If you've completed this sequence of tasks correctly, your computer should power up and you'll see a series of status messages on the monitor, ending with the Windows desktop or logon screen.

Run through Windows Setup

If this is the first time you've turned on the computer, you might need to run through a brief setup routine at this point. You can't skip this step, but you can go through it pretty quickly. Each screen asks you a question or allows you to select an option. The exact sequence of questions may vary slightly, depending on how the PC maker assembled your computer. Here's a list of what you can expect to accomplish as you complete this process:

- **Accept the End User License Agreement.** This is a legal agreement between you, the PC maker, and Microsoft setting out your legal rights to use the software. Most nonlawyers blow right by this lengthy document without giving it more than a cursory glance.

Special Instructions for Notebook Owners

If you have a portable PC, setting up your hardware is a bit easier. The monitor is an integral part of the package, so you don't need to worry about connecting it to the computer. Although you can use an external keyboard or mouse, there's no need to do so at this point. In fact, of the concerns that you have to deal with when setting up a desktop PC, the only one that applies to a notebook is power. Make sure you insert a battery pack into your PC, and then connect the external power supply to an AC power source.

As a space- and weight-saving measure, some portable PCs are designed without a built-in CD or DVD drive. If that's the case for your small, light computer, you may need to connect an external drive to a USB port to perform some essential tasks that I cover later in this book.

I recommend that you resist the temptation to unplug your portable PC and run on batteries while you're first getting set up. Some setup tasks will fail, with unpredictable results, if you run out of juice midway through. You'll have plenty of time to go "unplugged" after you make sure everything is working properly.

- **Enter your name and company name.** If this is a home computer, just enter your name again in the space for a company name.

- **Choose region/language/keyboard settings.** This choice tells Windows what language you want it to use for menus and dialog boxes. You can also specify that you're using a keyboard other than the U.S. American model. (Western European keyboards, for instance, offers keys and combinations that allow you to more easily enter accented characters.) If you're in the United States, you'll probably accept the defaults.

- **Select your time zone.** Scroll through the list and find the closest major city that's in your time zone. If your part of the world doesn't spring forward and fall back, make sure the **Daylight Saving Time** check box is clear. (If you're located in Arizona or Hawaii, the preconfigured time zone settings should do this automatically for you.)

- **Give your computer a name.** Whatever you enter here is what other people will see when they share your files or printers over a network. You can enter an optional description here as well, to make it easier to figure out which computer is which. Choose your computer name carefully, because it's difficult to change later without jumping through a bunch of hoops. You can choose something poetic if you want, like the name of a Greek god or your favorite beach resort. Don't fill in your user name as the name of the computer; if you do, Windows may get confused later when you try to set up a network. Windows will automatically create a random computer name for you, consisting of your last name (as entered in the Registered User setting) plus a series of random letters and numbers. If you're not feeling creative, feel free to use this suggested name.

  CAUTION Your computer name shows up in the headers of e-mail messages you send to other people. If you're concerned about protecting your privacy, avoid using any part of your name or your company name in your computer's name.

- **Activate and/or register your copy of Windows with Microsoft.** This step is optional. In fact, I want you to skip it for now, because we're not going to set up Internet access yet.

- **Set up Internet access.** You probably noticed that I didn't have you plug in your network card or modem earlier. That was deliberate. We'll get to this task later, when we can pay attention to important security precautions. For now, just tell Windows you want to skip this step.

- **Set up a user account.** By default, Windows XP creates an account called Administrator (or Owner, if you're using Windows XP Home Edition). The purpose of this account, as you might guess from the name, is to perform administrative tasks. For your regular, day-to-day computing, you should set up an account using your own name. I suggest that you enter your first name and avoid using any spaces. You can set up additional accounts for other people who will use your computer (your spouse or kids, for instance) now or wait until later.

You may encounter some additional screens as well, offering to help you set up an AOL or MSN account, for instance—don't do it yet—or configure some software that was bundled with your computer. When you've dealt with all the setup screens, click **Finish**. Your computer restarts, and you're ready to move on. At the Welcome screen, click the name of your user account (the one you just created) to continue to the Windows desktop.

☐ Take inventory: hardware

Did you actually get all the hardware you paid for? Now's a good time to check. You don't need to take the cover off the computer to see what's inside. Instead, get out your hardware packing slip, and we'll use some handy Windows tools to make sure all the pieces are present and accounted for. (If you encounter problems with any of the procedures listed here, see the Troubleshooting section at the end of this chapter.) Your most useful diagnostic tool is the System Properties dialog box, which you access like so:

1   Click **Start**.

2   On the Start menu, point to the My Computer icon near the top of the right column, and right-click.

3   Click **Properties**.

The General tab of the System Properties dialog box, shown here, displays a wealth of information about your computer:

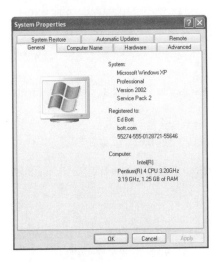

Start with the **processor**. This is the chip that acts as the brains of your computer. A faster chip means you can do more work in less time. In this case, my computer is powered by an Intel Pentium 4, running at a speed of 3.2 gigahertz (GHz). Your computer may use a different Intel processor, such as the Celeron, or it may use a chip from AMD instead. Just make sure it matches what you see on the packing slip.

Random access memory (RAM) is the single most important piece of the PC, in my opinion. The more memory you have, the more tasks you can do at the same time. The System Properties dialog box shows you how much RAM is installed on your computer. RAM is measured in megabytes or gigabytes. (1 GB is equal to approximately 1024 MB.) Most new computers these days come with at

NOTE Leave this dialog box open; you'll need it in the next section. You can slide it aside temporarily if it gets in your way.

least 256 MB of RAM, and it's not uncommon to find 512 MB or more. In the example shown here, I have 1.25 GB of RAM. If your computer has less than 256 MB of RAM, you should strongly consider upgrading now, before you go any further. Memory upgrades are cheap and easy to install.

Most new computers come with a single **hard disk**, on which you store programs and data files. If you collect digital music files or plan to transfer video files to your computer, you need lots and lots of disk space. To see how much is available on your computer, follow these steps:

1 Click **Start** and then **My Computer**.

2 Point to the icon for your main hard disk drive (typically identified as drive C:), right-click, and choose **Properties**.

3 Click the General tab of the properties dialog box for this disk.

Figure 2 depicts a disk drive that has a total capacity of 39 GB, of which only 6 GB is in use.

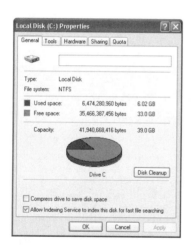

NOTE Don't be too concerned if the capacity of the drive on the packing slip is slightly different from the value you see here. Every disk-drive maker calculates capacity in a slightly different way. A 39-GB drive, originally sold as a 40-GB drive, may actually contain 41.9 million bytes. The capacities you see here may be lower than what you were sold. As long as the numbers are reasonably close to each another, they're OK.

Figure 2   *The text above the pie chart shown here tells you the actual capacity of your disk drive.*

If your computer includes a **floppy disk drive** (many modern computers do not), check to make sure it's working properly. Slide a floppy disk into the drive, click **Start**, click **My Computer**, and double-click the icon to view a list of files on the disk.

Finally, check your **CD/DVD drive** to make sure it's working properly. Press the button on the outside to open the drive tray, pop in a music CD, and push to close the tray again. If all goes well, your default music program should start automatically and begin playing music. If the music program doesn't begin automatically, click **Start**, click **My Computer**, and double-click the icon for your CD drive to begin playing the CD.

Take inventory: software

TIP   If you're comfortable with technical settings, this is a good time to learn how to access your computer's BIOS—the place where your PC stores detailed configuration information. Typically, you access the BIOS menus by tapping a key early in the boot process—the F2 and F10 function keys are popular choices for this job. If you're lucky, the boot screen includes a reminder of exactly which key to press to get into the BIOS; if not, you'll need to look it up in the computer's manual. Looking through the BIOS is an excellent way to ensure that your memory, hard disks, and other devices are installed correctly. This is also the place to specify where you want the computer to look for startup files. Before you can start the computer using your Windows XP CD (to set up or repair Windows), you may need to move the CD drive ahead of your hard disk in the list of boot devices.

Do you know what software is installed on your computer? Typically, a new PC comes with a bundle of programs in addition to Windows itself. I'll talk about those other programs later. For now, your goal is to capture a few details about your Windows version and to make sure that you have some important information safely stored away.

To determine which version of Windows is installed on your computer, use the System Properties dialog box. It should still be open; if it isn't, click **Start**, right-click **My Computer**, and click **Properties**. Two blocks of information at the top of the General tab are important:

- The **System** heading tells you which Windows version—Home Edition or Professional—is installed on your computer. If a Service Pack is installed, it's also noted here.

● Under **Registered To**, you should see your name and company name. If your PC maker filled in this information with generic information, however, you might see a name such as Valued Customer here. There's no easy way to change the name displayed here, unfortunately, unless you're comfortable editing the Registry.

NOTE The Windows Registry is a database that stores every detail of your computer's configuration. When you install a new program or add a new hardware device, for instance, the details go here. Although Windows XP includes a Registry Editor utility, you shouldn't need to edit the Registry directly except for specialized cases. If you want to learn more about the Registry and how it works, pick up a copy of *Microsoft Windows XP Inside Out, Second Edition* (Microsoft Press, 2004), co-authored by Carl Siechert, Craig Stinson, and yours truly.

The last piece of information in this block is a 20-digit numeric serial number. You might think this number is important—it's not. Instead, you *really* need to make sure you find your Windows XP CD key and store it in a safe place. This key, which consists of 25 letters and numbers, is essential if you ever need to reinstall Windows XP on your computer. This key is unique to your copy of Windows XP, and without it you'll be unable to repair Windows should you need to do so in the future.

You'll find the CD key on the back of the CD case, on a sticker attached to your PC, or on a separate piece of paper that came with your CD. Find a safe place for it, and don't allow it to become separated from the CD. If you can't find this information anywhere, flip back to page 7, where I explain how to use the Keyfinder program to locate this crucial information.

TIP If you have serial numbers or product keys for other programs that came with your computer, make sure you keep those in a safe place as well. You'll thank me someday if your hard disk crashes or you encounter another problem that forces you to reinstall Windows and your software.

Check your hard disk format

The manufacturer of your PC chose a file system—either NTFS or FAT32—when your disk was originally formatted. I don't want to get into a lot of technobabble here, but it's important that you make sure your hard disk is formatted with NTFS, which is more reliable and more secure than FAT32. You can see which file system is currently in use by checking the properties dialog box for the disk, as described earlier in the "Take inventory: hardware" step. Figure 2 on page 44 shows a disk formatted with the NTFS file system. If you see NTFS on the properties dialog box for your disk, congratulations—you can skip to the next section. If this dialog box says your disk is formatted using FAT32, however, you need to *convert* the drive using the following procedure. (Sorry to make you open an old-fashioned command prompt, but there's no other way, honest.)

Before starting, open the disk properties dialog box and make a note of the volume label—the text in the box at the top of the General tab. (On many computers, this label is blank.) You'll need this information to complete the conversion.

CAUTION In this procedure, I assume you're converting your C: drive. If you have a single icon in the Hard Disk Drives section of your My Computer window, as practically everyone does, this procedure is correct for you. If you see multiple icons here, check the drive letter in parentheses at the end of the label for the drive icon you're going to convert. If necessary, substitute a different drive letter in step 3.

1 Click **Start** and then click **Run**.

2 Click in the Open box, enter cmd, and press Enter.

3 Click in the Command Prompt window, and type the following command: convert c: /fs:ntfs. Press Enter.

4 When prompted for a volume label, type the name you noted earlier and press Enter. (If the volume label is blank, just press Enter.)

5 If you are converting the C: drive, which holds your Windows files, you'll see an error message that warns you the drive is in use and offers to dismount the drive for you. Press N to refuse this offer.

6 The next prompt offers to schedule the conversion to occur the next time you start Windows. Press Y and then Enter to accept this option.

Restart the computer. You'll see a prompt that warns you that the conversion is about to begin and gives you 10 seconds to cancel the conversion. If you allow it to proceed, Windows checks your disk for errors and completes the conversion. During this process, your computer will restart twice.

Set up a user account for each person who uses your PC

You might have already completed this task when you ran through the "out of the box" Windows Setup routine earlier. If you skipped it then, now's your chance to add another user account (or two or three).

Every person who uses your computer should have his or her own account. That way, all of you can keep your private files private, you can decorate your desktop with your favorite colors and photos without worrying that someone else will undo your work, and you can each keep tabs on your own e-mail.

An even more important reason to set up individual user accounts is for the sake of security. Windows XP allows you to set up two types of accounts:

- With a **Computer Administrator** account, you have full rights and privileges over the computer. With this type of account, you can install programs, manage files and folders, and create new accounts or change existing ones.

- Using a **Limited** account, you can run programs that have already been installed on the computer and make some changes to your own account, but you can't install new programs, access other people's files, or change other user accounts.

A Limited account is an ideal solution when you want a child to have access to your computer. They're less likely to cause problems, accidentally or deliberately, and they won't be able to install spyware or allow a virus to sneak onto the computer.

Here's how to create a new account:

1 Click **Start**, and then click **Control Panel**.

2 Double-click **User Accounts**.

3 In the User Accounts dialog box, click **Create a new account**.

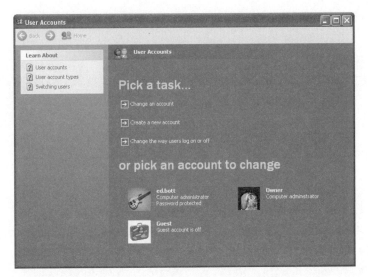

4 Enter a name for the new user. This is the name that appears on the Welcome screen and at the top of the Start menu after you log on. Click **Next** to continue.

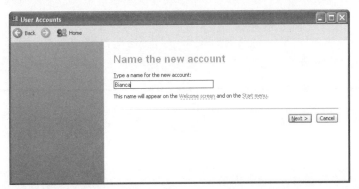

5 Choose an account type, **Computer Administrator** or **Limited**.

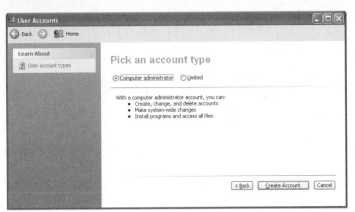

6   Click **Create Account**.

You now return to the User Accounts dialog box, where you can repeat these steps to create additional accounts, if you wish. When you're all done, check this item off the list and move on.

☐ Add a password to your user account

When you create a user account during the initial "out of the box" Windows setup routine, you don't get a chance to create a password. After you start your computer for the first time, your user account remains unprotected. Anyone who sits in front of your computer can click your name on the Welcome screen to log on to your account and start working with existing programs; installing new ones; or creating, changing, and deleting files.

No matter how much you trust the people around you, I recommend that you create a password for your account. Doing so increases your security noticeably, and it lessens the chance that another user will accidentally log on to your account and mess with your files or settings.

Your password doesn't have to be complicated. Ideally, it should be at least seven characters long, with a mix of capital and lowercase letters and numbers. It should be easy for you to remember and hard for someone else to guess—that means no using your pet's name or your birthday!

To create a new password, follow these steps:

1   Open Control Panel, double-click **User Accounts**, and click **Change an Account**.

2   Click your account name in the User Accounts dialog box.

3   Click **Create a password**.

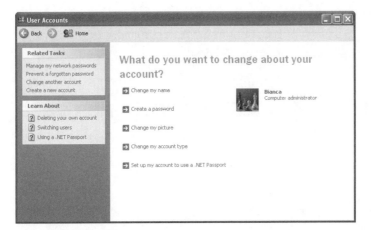

4   In the **Create a password for your account** dialog box, type the new password in
    both boxes. (Typing the password twice is a security precaution that prevents you
    from accidentally mistyping your intended password and being unable to access
    your account later.)

5   If you want to add a hint to remind yourself of the password, you can enter a word
    or phrase in the box at the bottom. This hint is available from the Welcome screen
    if you get stuck. Click **Next** to continue.

    Remember, anyone can see the password hint, so don't make it too easy to guess.
    The hint should be something that will jog your memory but won't help someone
    who's trying to break into your computer.

6   Click **Create Password**.

7   At this point, Windows offers you an opportunity to make your files private so that only you can read them. I prefer this option on my own computer, but you can safely choose either option, after which you'll be returned to the User Accounts dialog box.

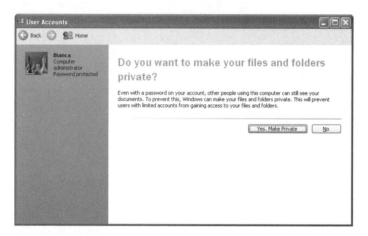

8   Click **Start**, then click **Log Off**. Return to the Welcome screen, click your user name, and enter the new password to verify that it works.

Create a password reset disk

I don't know about you, but my memory isn't what it used to be, and trying to keep track of dozens of passwords and PINs puts a strain on my poor, overworked brain cells. Although it's possible to log on with the Administrator account to reset your password if you just can't remember it, there's a better solution: create a password reset disk. This disk stores a copy of your password in an encrypted format that no one can read. If your memory completely fails you and you're unable to enter the correct password at the Welcome screen, you can insert the disk and create a new password.

To create this indispensable tool, you need a floppy disk or a USB flash memory key. Insert the disk into the drive or plug the memory key into a USB port, and then follow these steps:

1   Click **Start**, click **Control Panel**, and double-click **User Accounts**.

2   In the User Accounts dialog box, click the name of your account.

3 At the left side of the **What do you want to change about your account?** box, under the **Related Tasks** heading, click **Prevent a forgotten password**. This starts the Forgotten Password wizard.

4 After reading the introductory screen, click **Next** to continue.

5 In the **Create a Password Reset Disk** dialog box, select the drive where you want to save the password reset files. Click **Next**.

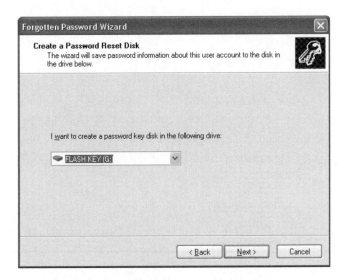

6 In the **Current User Account Password** dialog box, enter your current password and click **Next**.

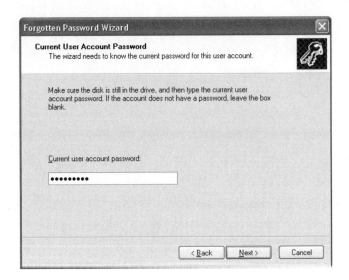

7 The following two screens are strictly informational, providing progress indicators and letting you know when the disk is complete.

8 After completing the wizard, remove the disk, label it clearly, and store it in a safe place.

If you ever forget your password, click in the box on the Welcome screen where you normally type your password and press Enter. Then click the **Use Your Password Reset Disk** link, and follow the instructions.

Test and troubleshoot

Most new computers are thoroughly tested (a process called "burning in") before they're delivered to a customer. But a lot can happen between the factory and your desk. If you encounter problems during the initial stages of setting up your computer, the most likely cause is that something rattled loose during transit. Here are some possible solutions to common problems:

- **Problem: Your computer reports that you have less memory than you expect.**
  Solution: *Turn the computer off first.* Then remove the computer cover and look at the RAM chips in the memory slots. One or more may have come loose during shipment. Try reseating the memory chips by pressing down firmly but gently.

- **Problem: Your display is jumpy or flickers.**
  Solution: This could be caused by a display adapter that has jiggled loose from its slot. *Turn the computer off first.* Remove the cover, find the slot that contains the video card, and press down firmly to snap the card into the slot.

- **Problem: A floppy disk or CD drive doesn't work properly.** Solution: *Turn the computer off first.* Remove the cover and look for loose connections. Each drive has two connectors, one that brings power to the drive, the other connecting the drive to the motherboard. Press firmly on each connection to make sure the connections are snug and secure.

CAUTION Your PC is filled with sensitive parts, and it's connected to an AC power supply. If you accidentally unseat a card or memory chip while the PC is powered up, or if you discharge a burst of static electricity into a chip, you could inadvertently destroy that part and render your computer useless. You could slice off a finger in a fast-moving fan, and the power supply could give you a jolt that could knock you across the room. The moral of the story? Turn off the power before you open the cover, and be extremely careful when working with your PC's innards.

- **Problem: Your computer shuts down or produces errors intermittently.** Solution: This type of problem can be maddening to troubleshoot, but the number-one culprit is heat. Remove the cover and power up the computer; then carefully check the fans on the CPU chip and at the front and back of the computer to make sure they're working properly. If all appears to be in order, return the computer to the manufacturer to check for a defective CPU or memory chip.

- **Problem: One or more hardware devices don't work properly.** Solution: If a DVD drive refuses to play DVDs or a video card won't display a good-looking image, the problem might be a missing or defective device driver—a piece of software that allows the device to work with Windows. Call the manufacturer, and ask them to walk you through a suitable diagnostics routine.

Step 2: **Protect Your PC**

It's a sad fact of modern life: every time you switch on your PC, you expose yourself to security risks. Viruses and worms can strike when you least expect them, and they can go undetected indefinitely if you don't know the warning signs. If an attacker succeeds in taking over your computer with a Trojan horse program, he can tap your bank accounts, steal your identity, and use your computer as a "zombie" to transmit spam or attack other computers.

If you think you're immune, that no one could possibly be interested in the humdrum contents of your hard drive, think again. It *can* happen to you. Hackers, data thieves, and online vandals are indiscriminate in their attacks. Your job is to avoid getting caught in their snares. Fortunately, protecting yourself and your PC doesn't require an advanced technical degree in cybersecurity—just some common sense and a healthy respect for your online surroundings.

In this chapter, I'll show you how to install and configure some essential security tools, starting with the most important one of all, Windows XP Service Pack 2 (SP2). Throughout this book, I assume that you've installed SP2. If you haven't, some of my advice will make no sense. More importantly, your computer will be exposed to unacceptable security risks. The steps I outline in this chapter will make sure you have a high level of protection.

✓ Checklist:

❑ **Establish a baseline level of security (page 58).** Before you connect to the Internet, make sure you have the built-in Microsoft Windows firewall up and running.

❑ **Set up a high-speed Internet connection (page 59).** Good news: the Network Setup Wizard will do most of the work for you.

❑ **Configure a dial-up Internet connection (page 63).** A different wizard will walk you through the process of getting your dial-up connection online. Have your password handy.

❑ **Get the latest Windows updates (page 69).** Before you do anything else, make sure Windows XP Service Pack 2 is installed. Then visit Windows Update for the most recent batch of security patches and critical updates.

❑ **Check your security settings (page 70).** Use the Windows Security Center (new in SP2) to make sure important security features are enabled.

❑ **Install antivirus software (page 71).** You can't afford to be without this essential protection from viruses, worms, and other Internet dangers.

❑ **Get the latest antivirus updates (page 72).** For effective protection, make sure you're set up to receive automatic updates on the latest online threats.

❑ **Turn on the Windows Firewall (page 75).** You should disable this feature if you choose to use a third-party software firewall instead.

❑ **Set up Automatic Updates (page 77).** Windows will automatically download the latest updates as soon as they're ready; you can choose how you want to install the updates after they arrive.

❑ **Protect your privacy (page 79).** Block bad cookies, allow good ones, and put a stop to unwanted pop-up windows.

☐ Establish a baseline level of security

Computer security is a tricky thing. As many users of Windows discovered when the Blaster worm appeared several years ago, viruses and worms can jump onto your computer over an Internet connection. You don't have to open an e-mail message or double-click a file—just going online with an unprotected connection may be enough to expose you to a dangerous program that can shut down your computer, delete files, or allow an attacker to take over your PC. You're at an even higher level of risk when using a computer on which critical updates to Windows haven't been installed.

But here's the catch. To install those critical updates, you have to connect to the Internet. But if you connect to the Internet before installing those updates, you risk getting clobbered by a worm. How do you stay secure? By making sure that you have a working *firewall* before you go online. Before you even think about plugging in that Internet connection, let's make sure you've established this essential baseline level of security. Here's how:

1   Click **Start**, right-click the My Computer icon, click **Properties**, and look at the text under **System**, on the General tab.

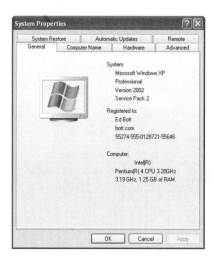

- If you see **Service Pack 2** in this description, you don't need to do any more. The Windows Firewall is enabled, and you can skip ahead to the next section, "Set up a high-speed Internet connection."

- If you see **Service Pack 1** or no reference at all to a service pack, continue with this procedure.

2   Click **Start**, click **Control Panel**, and click **Network and Internet Connections**. (If this option isn't available and you see a folder filled with icons, click **Switch to Category View** in the **Control Panel** task list on the left.).

3   Click **Network Connections**.

- If the Network Connections folder is empty, or if you see connections only under the **Dial-up** heading, you can skip ahead to the "Configure a dial-up Internet connection" section on page 63.

- If you see a Local Area Connection icon, continue with this procedure.

4   Right-click the Local Area Connection icon, and click **Properties**.

5   On the Advanced tab, click to select the **Internet Connection Firewall** check box. (If you see a **Windows Firewall** section here, with a **Settings** button alongside it, you have Service Pack 2 installed and you can stop here.)

6   Click **OK** to close this dialog box, but leave the Network Connections folder open for the next step.

TIP   The ideal way to install SP2 on your new PC is to use an "official" CD from Microsoft. Although you can order the SP2 CD from Microsoft, it might take weeks to arrive, and you probably don't want to wait that long. If you know someone who has this CD, you can borrow their copy—the CD is designed to work on any computer running any version of Windows XP.

Set up a high-speed Internet connection

Your new PC works best when you hook it up to a high-speed Internet connection (sometimes also referred to as a *broadband connection*). Typically, this type of Internet connection is supplied over the same cable that carries your TV (with a cable modem) or over phone wires (using *digital subscriber line*, or DSL, technology). High-speed Internet connections have become increasingly popular in recent years. In the United States, they're now more common than dial-up connections.

TIP   If you're currently using a dial-up connection and you have the opportunity to upgrade to broadband, I strongly recommend that you do so. Besides the convenience and speed of having a fast connection that's always available, the biggest advantage is that you can take full advantage of the Automatic Updates feature in Windows XP. That's an important step on the road to making sure your computer is secure.

The exact hardware you'll need to make your new PC work with a high-speed Internet connection varies, and you should check the details with your Internet service provider. For this set of instructions, I assume you're using the most common configuration, which is illustrated in Figure 1 and which consists of the following elements:

- **External cable or DSL modem.** This box is connected to a phone jack (DSL) or to a cable outlet (cable modem). It also has an RJ-45 jack, which is similar (but not identical) in size and shape to a telephone adapter. This jack, shown here, is where you'll connect the external modem to your computer or network:

- **Network adapter.** Also known as an Ethernet adapter, this is usually an internal component of your computer. It also has an RJ-45 jack.

- **Network cable(s) with RJ-45 connectors at either end.** If you have a single computer connected to the Internet, you need a single cable that directly connects the network adapter to your cable or DSL modem. If you want to share your high-speed connection with one or more additional computers, you need to add one more component.

- **Router.** This component, which is essential for a network, has one RJ-45 jack that connects to your high-speed modem (typically this is called the *wide area network*, or WAN, connector) and several RJ-45 connectors that connect to Ethernet adapters. (You can read more details about routers in the next chapter, beginning on page 84.)

NOTE If you want to add a wireless computer to your network (or if you think you might want to do so in the future), look for a router that has both wired ports and a wireless access point integrated into it. This type of router costs a little more than a wired-only version, but it's convenient to have all these capabilities in one box.

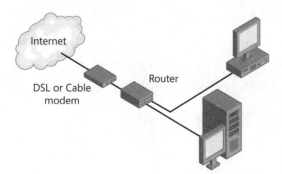

Figure 1 *These are the building blocks of a high-speed network. If you have only one computer, you can remove the router and connect your PC directly to the modem.*

You may need a service technician to make the connection to the Internet, although an increasing number of ISPs offer do-it-yourself connection kits. After you set up the cable or DSL modem, use a network cable to connect the modem to the WAN port on your router, and then use a second cable to connect the network adapter in your computer to a LAN port on the router. (If you're not installing a router, just use a single cable to connect your network adapter to the RJ-45 port on the cable modem.)

You're now ready to run the Network Setup Wizard. On the left side of the Network Connections folder, under the heading **Network Tasks**, click **Set up a home or small office network**. The precise steps of the wizard vary from computer to computer, depending on what type of network hardware

NOTE Don't let the name confuse you—you should use the Network Setup Wizard even if you have only a single computer and you don't plan to set up a local area network. Look at it this way: the Internet is the world's biggest network, and this is the best way to configure your connection to that network so that you stay secure.

you've installed and whether you've set up Service Pack 2 yet. Follow the wizard's prompts; the text in each dialog box does a good job of explaining your options. Most of the dialog boxes in this wizard contain links that lead to additional information; if you get confused about which option to choose, click the link and read more.

Here are some things to look out for when completing the Network Setup Wizard:

- If you have a router that was designed to work with Windows XP and you have SP2 installed, you'll see a dialog box like the one shown here. Click the first option (**Yes, use the existing shared connection...**).

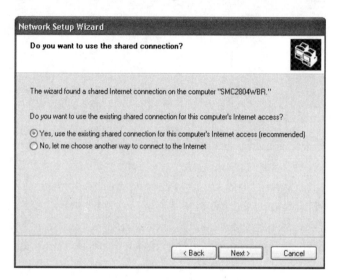

- The wizard asks you to confirm your computer's name. This dialog box shows the current name of the computer and includes a box where you can enter a description. The description is useful if you're planning to set up a network and you want other people on the network to know that this is your computer when they see it in the My Network Places folder.

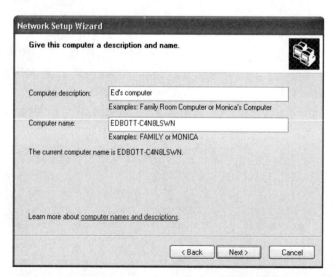

- The SP2 version of the Network Setup Wizard asks if you want to enable file and printer sharing. Choose whichever option you prefer. If you change your mind, you can always run the wizard again.

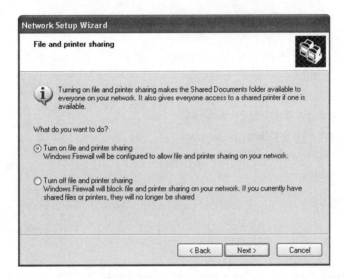

- In its final step, the wizard offers you the chance to create a disk you can use to set up other computers on your local network. If you have a Windows XP CD, you don't need this disk; if you don't have a CD, create the Network Setup disk and put it aside. You'll use it later.

You should now have a working Internet connection. To test it, open Internet Explorer and visit the default home page. I know you'll be tempted at this point to browse a few more Web pages or check your e-mail, but don't do it yet! We still need to take care of some additional security steps.

CAUTION If you have a local area network, don't set it up now. Wait until you've finished updating your computer. You'll get a chance to do several network-related tasks in "Step 3: Get Connected," which begins on page 84.

You can now skip ahead to "Get the latest Windows updates," on page 69.

Configure a dial-up Internet connection

Broadband connections are the best for many reasons, but for some people they're simply not available. If your only option for Internet access is a dial-up connection, you'll need to set things up properly. The procedures I describe here also apply if you're using a dial-up connection as your secondary Internet connection. This is especially true if you have a notebook computer that normally connects to a broadband network at home. Here is a brief summary of what you need to accomplish:

- **Set up your modem.** If your new PC came with an internal modem that's compatible with Windows XP, this task should be done already, thanks to the miracle of Windows Plug and Play. You can also use an external modem that plugs into a USB or serial port. Connect the modem port to your phone jack by using a standard telephone cable.

  > **TIP** If you're having troubles with your modem, help is just a click or two away. Click Start, and then click Help and Support. In the **Search** box, type **troubleshoot modem** and click the green search arrow to the right of the box. In the **Search Results** list, click the "Troubleshooting Modems" topic and follow the instructions.

- **Enter your connection settings, and save them for reuse.** At a minimum, you need to enter the phone number you use for access, your user name, and your password.

- **Secure the connection.** Many people mistakenly believe that accessing the Internet over a dial-up connection is somehow safer than doing the same tasks over a high-speed connection. Dial-up connections may be slower and the connections temporary by nature, but a virus, worm, or Trojan horse program doesn't discriminate by connection speed. Dial-up users need to be conscious of computer security—period.

- **Configure Windows to use your dial-up connection.** You can set the connection to dial automatically whenever you go online, or you can specify that you only want to go online when you specifically choose to do so. (This option is useful if you pay by the minute for Internet access and don't want any surprises on your bill!)

The good news is that a wizard (yes, another one) handles most of the difficult tasks for you. Connect your modem to the phone line, and let's get started.

Click **Start**, click **Control Panel**, and click **Network and Internet Connections**. Under the **Pick a task...** heading, click **Set up or change your Internet connection**. This opens the Internet Properties dialog box and displays the Connections tab. Click **Setup** to start the New Connection Wizard. Click **Next** to move past the welcome page, and then follow the wizard's prompts to set up your connection.

1 On the **Network Connection Type** page, choose **Connect to the Internet** and click **Next**.

2 On the **Getting Ready** page, choose **Set up my connection manually** and click **Next**.

3 On the **Internet Connection** page, choose **Connect using a dial-up modem** and click **Next**.

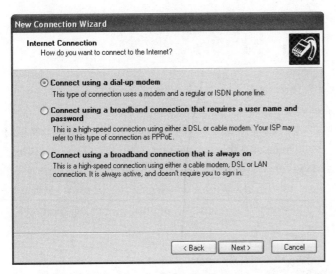

4 On the **Connection Name** page, click in the text box and type a name for your connection. This is the name that will appear on a **Connect To** menu added to the Start button and under the connection icon in the My Network Places folder. Click **Next**.

TIP   When naming a dial-up connection, I recommend that you use a descriptive name, such as My Earthlink Connection. Add a city name or other identifier if you're creating icons for use on a notebook, where the connection settings change depending on where you're staying.

5 On the **Phone Number to Dial** page, enter your access number, exactly as you would dial it. If you're calling from a hotel or an office, you may need to enter a 9 first. If you're calling a number outside your home area, you might have to enter a 1 and/or an area code. Add a comma to insert a pause after any number. Click **Next** to continue.

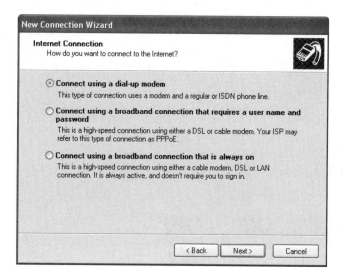

6   On the **Internet Account Information** page, enter your user name and password. (You'll need to enter your password a second time to verify that you didn't accidentally strike the wrong key in the first text box.) If you don't want other people who use your computer to have access to this connection, clear the top check box, **Use this account name and password when anyone connects to the Internet from this computer**. Clear the bottom check box, **Make this the default Internet connection**, if you're creating a second connection that you will not normally use for Internet access. Click **Next**.

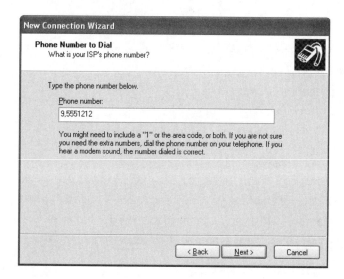

7   The final page of the wizard confirms that you entered everything correctly. If you prefer to go online by clicking an icon, click **Add a shortcut to this connection to my desktop**. Click **Finish** to create the connection.

Repeat this process if you want to create and save a second dial-up connection. You might want two or more connection icons if you have a choice of local access numbers, one of which is sometimes busy, or if you travel to several locations on a regular basis and want quick access to the Internet via the modem on your notebook PC.

When you create a dial-up connection on a computer running SP2, Windows adds a **Connect To** choice to the Start menu and enables the Windows Firewall for that connection. To verify that the connection is protected, click **Start**, click **Connect To,** and click **Show All Connections**. Figure 2 shows what a connection icon looks like when you're not connected to the Internet.

Figure 2   *The black check mark indicates this is a default connection, and the text tells you the connection is protected by the Windows Firewall.*

If you don't see **Firewalled** alongside your connection icon, you'll need to manually enable the firewall protection. Right-click the icon, click **Properties**, and click the Advanced tab. If you're using Windows XP with Service Pack 1 or earlier, click to select the **Internet Connection Firewall** check box. If SP2 is already installed, click **Settings** under **Windows Firewall** and then click **On (Recommended).** Click **OK** to save the changes. Close both dialog boxes to continue.

Finally, change the settings that determine whether Windows automatically calls up your Internet connection when you browse the Web or use e-mail. To view—and, if necessary, adjust—these settings, open Internet Explorer, click **Tools**, and click **Internet Options**. Click the Connections tab to see the dialog box shown on the next page.

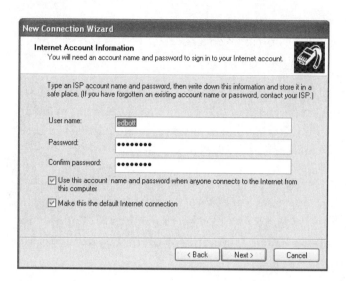

Three choices appear below the list of available dial-up connections:

- Click **Never dial a connection** if you want Windows to connect to the Internet only when you double-click the connection icon. Windows will not auto-dial with this setting enabled.

- Click **Dial whenever a network connection is not present** if you normally use a broadband connection but want Windows to automatically use a dial-up connection when the broadband connection isn't working. This configuration is most common on notebook computers.

What If You Use MSN or AOL?

The two largest providers of dial-up Internet access in the world are Microsoft's MSN and America Online (AOL). Both of these services work in ways that are substantially different from a conventional provider of dial-up Internet access. They use custom dialer programs, provide e-mail and Web pages through custom programs, and offer other features that are only available to subscribers.

If you use either one of these services as your primary route to the Internet, your best bet is to acquire the latest software on CD. If you install an older version of the software from either service, you'll need to download a large update over your dial-up connection—a process that can take a very long time.

- Click **Always dial my default connection** if you have only a dial-up connection *and* you have a dedicated phone line *and* you want Windows to automatically make a dial-up connection whenever it's needed.

CAUTION The **Always dial my default connection** option can get very expensive if you pay for Internet access by the hour (or the minute) and you leave your computer running while you're away. If any program is set to automatically access the Internet—if you've set up your e-mail program to check for messages every half-hour, say—you could spend much more time online than you intended.

☐ Get the latest Windows updates

You're connected to the Internet, and your firewall is enabled. Excellent—you're well on the way to having a secure computer. Now you need to make sure you have the latest updates for Windows XP. Here are your options:

- **If Service Pack 2 is already installed...** Visit Windows Update now—click **Start**, click **All Programs**, and then click **Windows Update**—and install the latest security patches and critical updates by using the **Express Install** option.

- **If Service Pack 2 is not installed...** Visit the Windows Update site now, and click the **Express Install** option. From the list of available updates, choose Service Pack 2. (This update must be installed independently of any other updates.) Windows will automatically download the Express version of SP2. Because this download is tailored specifically for your computer, it is considerably smaller than the full version. It's still quite large, however, taking up between 70 and 1 MB of disk space. Size won't be an issue over a high-speed Internet connection, but you might have to wait several hours to download SP2 completely over a dial-up connection. When SP2 is fully installed, restart your computer, visit Windows Update, and use the **Express Install** option to get any additional updates you might need.

TIP If you have a high-speed Internet connection and you have several computers running Windows XP, here's an alternate strategy. Visit *http://www.microsoft.com/security* and locate the link for the full download of Service Pack 2. This file is more than 260 MB in size, so download it *only* if you have a high-speed connection. Save the file in your Downloads folder, and double-click its icon to begin the installation. Copy the file to a CD, and install it on your other computers. You can also share the CD with friends and neighbors who use Windows XP and may not have installed SP2 yet.

Check your security settings

If you've used Windows XP before, you'll notice one important security-related improvement added by Service Pack 2—a new utility called the Windows Security Center. Its job is to monitor three crucial security settings to ensure that you're not vulnerable to security risks. If any of these settings have the potential to cause problems on your computer, you'll see a red or yellow shield icon and a balloon notification in the lower right corner of your screen, like the one shown here:

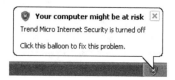

You can check the Windows Security Center manually at any time. Click **Start**, click **Control Panel**, and click **Security Center**. If the three items under **Security essentials** show a green ON icon, you're in good shape. If any of them are yellow or red, as in the example shown in Figure 3, you need to check the settings and make any necessary adjustments. The following sections discuss these items in more detail.

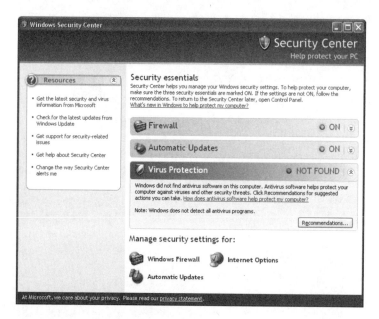

Figure 3   *If you see a red or yellow warning message in the Security Center, check it out completely—do not ignore these warnings!*

A yellow or red icon may not mean that you actually have a problem, only that Windows Security Center can't confirm that your settings are correct. You'll see a yellow icon if you set Automatic Updates to download new updates automatically but not install them until you give it the go-ahead. Similarly, a third-party firewall or antivirus program might not communicate its status to Windows Security Center, resulting in a red icon. When in doubt, check it out as fully as possible.

Install antivirus software

I don't need to tell you how destructive computer viruses can be. Over the past few years, outbreaks of fast-spreading worms and viruses aimed at computers running Windows have made headlines worldwide. You probably know at least one person who's been a virus victim; you may even have firsthand experience with the frustration and hassle of having to clean up after a virus infection. If you've personally been spared this grief so far, count your blessings, and then resolve to keep your system virus-free in the future.

Windows XP does not include any software that can detect viruses or clean up after a viral infection. With SP2 installed, Windows offers some important new protections that can block certain types of files that are often infected with viruses, but you'll need to turn to third-party software to provide more comprehensive protection. I can't imagine operating a computer without effective, up-to-date antivirus software, and neither should you.

TIP   Don't let a tight budget leave you unprotected. Microsoft's antivirus Web site—*http://www.microsoft.com/athome/security/protect/antivirus.mspx*—includes links to a number of effective antivirus programs with free trials ranging from 90 days to one full year in length. Try several until you find one that you feel is worth the cost. In the meantime, keep your eyes open for deals on antivirus software—software makers regularly offer generous rebates on security software, in some cases making the software free after you receive the rebate.

Many name-brand computers include a trial version of a popular antivirus program, which typically includes updates for a limited time. When the trial program ends, you have to purchase an update subscription or remove the program and install another.

CAUTION   Two antivirus programs are not better than one. In fact, having two such programs installed can cause all sorts of problems. If you decide to switch to a new antivirus program, don't install the new program until you completely remove the old one using the Add or Remove Programs option in Control Panel.

After you have successfully installed your antivirus program, you can move on to the next step.

❑ Get the latest antivirus updates

Simply installing an antivirus program is only the first step in protecting your computer from infections. Antivirus software typically works by scanning every new file you receive as an e-mail attachment or try to save to your hard disk. This scan compares the file's contents to the "signatures" contained in a database of known viruses. When the antivirus software detects a match, indicating that you've just received or downloaded a probable virus, it prevents you from executing or saving the infected file.

So far, so good. But what happens next week, when a new virus appears? If the database of known viruses doesn't include the signature of this new bug, your antivirus software might not detect it. If you then run the infected file, you'll be infected by the virus it contains.

This scenario isn't just a theoretical risk. Most of the new viruses that make headlines do so because they're able to spread themselves quickly and take advantage of people who have not yet updated their antivirus software to detect the new virus. How do you avoid being part of this group? Follow these steps:

1   After installing the antivirus software, run its update option immediately to install the latest antivirus signatures and any updates to the program itself.

2   After installing this first set of updates, run the update program again; some of the updates may in turn require updates of their own.

3   Follow the program's instructions to configure automatic updates.

Because each antivirus program uses its own procedures, you'll have to check your program's documentation to determine exactly how to download updates and set up automatic updates. The following are examples of how to accomplish this task using two popular antivirus programs.

To set update options using McAfee VirusScan 8.0, click **Start**, click **All Programs**, click **McAfee**, and then click **McAfee SecurityCenter**. In the McAfee SecurityCenter, shown in Figure 4, click **Updates** (in the upper right corner).

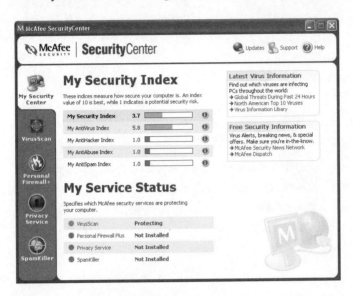

Figure 4   *If you use McAfee's antivirus software, visit this window to get the latest updates.*

When you see the SecurityCenter Updates dialog box shown here, click **Configure** to verify that the program is set to download updates automatically. This is the default setting in the McAfee Automatic Update Options dialog box.

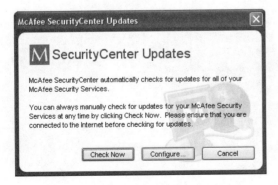

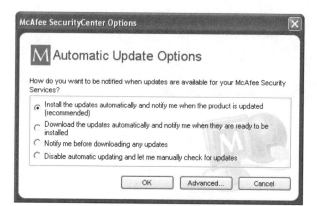

TIP If the manual update doesn't seem to work, a new security feature in Windows XP SP2 may have blocked the download and installation of the required ActiveX control. On the McAfee Web page, just below the Address bar, look for an Information Bar with a blue shield and yellow text that begins, This site might require the following ActiveX control... Click this bar to display an ActiveX menu, and then click **Install ActiveX Control...**

Finally, click **Check Now** to download and install the latest updates manually. This button takes you to a Web page that requires you to log on using the e-mail address and password you supplied when you first installed the program. You'll also need to install an ActiveX control to enable downloads, and you may need to restart your computer before completing the download.

If you use Symantec's Norton AntiVirus 2004, a utility called LiveUpdate checks for the latest updates and allows you to download future updates automatically. To check for updates manually, click **Start**, click **All Programs**, click **Norton AntiVirus**, and then click **Norton AntiVirus 2004**. In the Norton AntiVirus control panel, shown in Figure 5, click **LiveUpdate** to check for any updates and install them automatically.

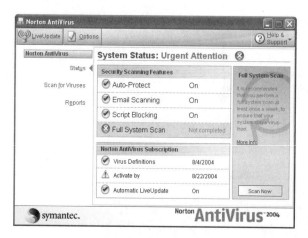

Figure 5 *Norton AntiVirus uses the LiveUpdate utility to update itself regularly.*

To configure LiveUpdate, open the main Norton AntiVirus window and click **Options**. In the left pane, click **LiveUpdate** to display the dialog box shown below. Make sure that the check box to the left of **Enable automatic LiveUpdate (recommended)** is selected. Click **OK** to accept these options.

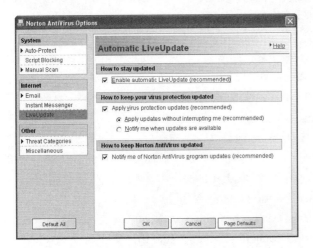

☐ Turn on the Windows Firewall

Firewalls are a crucial part of the "armor" that protects you from outside attacks. Windows XP has always included a firewall that prevents another computer (on your network or on the Internet) from making an unsolicited connection to your computer. The original release of Windows XP included the Internet Connection Firewall (ICF). Unfortunately, it caused problems with some programs and networks. And because this firewall was disabled by default, most Windows XP users never knew it existed.

SP2 replaces the old ICF with an all-new program called the Windows Firewall. It works well with other programs and networks, and it's turned on by default. If you've followed the instructions up to this point, you should see a green icon next to the Firewall category in Security Center.

I recommend that you leave the Windows Firewall on, using its default settings, unless one of the following conditions is true:

- **You've installed a third-party firewall program.** These days, many antivirus programs are included as part of a larger, full-featured security package. If you chose this option when you installed your antivirus software, you may have also installed a firewall component that adds bells and whistles not included in the bare-bones Windows Firewall. If you decide to keep using the separate firewall program, the Windows Firewall can interfere with its proper operation. In that case, you should disable the Windows Firewall. If you find the third-party firewall program too restrictive or complicated, you can disable it, at which point you'll need to reenable the Windows Firewall.

  CAUTION Some computer experts insist that you need to replace the Windows Firewall with a more powerful third-party software firewall so that you can detect spyware programs in action. What they don't tell you is that a more powerful firewall can also be nightmarish to set up, and some of your favorite programs may appear to stop working when the firewall becomes a little *too* protective. Unless you're a certified expert on networking software, I recommend that you stick with the Windows Firewall. If you choose a third-party replacement and some of your programs behave strangely, check the firewall settings first when troubleshooting.

- **You have one or more programs that are blocked by the firewall's default settings.** Windows will automatically configure most programs to work correctly through the firewall. When you first use a program that accesses the Internet, the Windows Firewall prompts you to block or unblock that program. In some rare cases, you might find that a favorite online game or file-transfer program doesn't work properly. In that case, you might need to tweak the Windows Firewall configuration.

To enable, disable, or reconfigure the Windows Firewall, open Security Center (click **Start**, click **Control Panel**, and click **Security Center**) and click the Windows Firewall icon at the bottom of the dialog box. This opens the dialog box shown here:

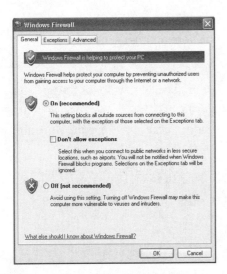

TIP   The check box to the left of Don't allow exceptions is normally unselected. You should click here only if you want to set security to its highest level. This would be appropriate if you suspect that you may be vulnerable to a new, fast-spreading worm that your antivirus software cannot detect yet. It is also a good idea to check this box if you use a wireless Internet connection in a public place (such as your local coffee shop), where other users might be able to attempt to hack into your portable PC.

On the General tab, Click **Off (not recommended)** to turn off the Windows Firewall. Click **On (recommended)** to reenable the Windows Firewall.

If you regularly play a multiplayer game that uses your network or the Internet, you might need to adjust firewall settings on the Exceptions tab to allow incoming connections to work properly. (We'll get to the details of this task in "Reinstall your favorite programs," beginning on page 152.)

Set up Automatic Updates

Earlier in this step, you installed the latest updates for Windows. Now, how do you make sure you get the next batch of updates when it's ready? That's the purpose of the Automatic Updates feature. When you install SP2, Windows forces you to choose a setting for this feature; if you accept the default settings, a small program runs in the background, regularly checking for new updates that you haven't yet installed. Each new update is downloaded automatically, during times when your computer isn't busy with other things. When the download is complete, Windows installs the updates automatically, restarting your computer if necessary.

This option is the safest way to ensure that you never miss an important update. Microsoft recommends this option, and for most people it is absolutely the best way to configure your system. However, what happens if you leave a document open and unsaved at the end of the day? If Windows decides to install an automatic update and restart your computer at 3:00 AM (the default time), you risk losing your unsaved data.

I prefer to adjust this setting so that Windows automatically downloads the updates for me and notifies me that they're ready to be installed. (The notification appears in the lower right corner of the screen, near the clock.) I can then save my work and restart my computer to install the updates.

To set this option, open Security Center and click the Automatic Updates icon. In the Automatic Updates dialog box, click **Download updates for me, but let me choose when to install them**.

CAUTION Your computer's security should be a top priority. Unfortunately, it's human nature to get distracted or to ignore the notification that a new update has been downloaded and say, "I'll get to that later." When you see an update notification, pay attention to it. Usually, installation takes only a few minutes; don't postpone the update any longer than you have to. Postponing an update puts you at a greater risk of falling victim to security problems. If you don't want to be bothered by these prompts, get in the habit of saving your work when you leave your computer each night, and leave the Automatic Updates option at its default setting.

After you make this change, the Automatic Updates entry in Windows Security Center will no longer display a green icon; instead, it displays a yellow **Check Settings** label. Don't be alarmed. This is perfectly normal and simply means that you've chosen not to use the recommended setting.

Protect your privacy

So far, everything you've done in this chapter has been aimed at preventing truly terrible things from happening to your computer. Windows XP includes a group of settings, most of them new in SP2, aimed at protecting your privacy and preventing unwanted interruptions when you surf the Internet. The two features you'll configure here affect two features of Internet Explorer:

- **How should Internet Explorer handle cookies?** These small text files record information when you visit a specific Web site; the Web site can read the information stored in that cookie the next time you visit a page on that site. Some cookies are tremendously useful. These "good" cookies allow you to automatically log on with a user name and password at your local newspaper's Web site, for instance. Cookies are also used to keep track of which items you've added to an online shopping cart. "Bad" cookies are those that can be used to keep a running list of which sites you visit on the Internet, potentially allowing a third party to make judgments about your interests or preferences that might not be justified. Your goal is to allow cookies that are useful and don't represent a threat to your privacy while blocking all others.

- **Do you want to block pop-up windows?** Mostly, pop-ups are just annoying, but they can also be dangerous. Not all pop-ups are bad. For instance, some sites use pop-ups to display a logon dialog box or to show photos or detailed information when you click a link in an online product catalog. However, some unscrupulous Web site designers use pop-ups as a way to fool unsophisticated users into installing dangerous software or clicking links that could lead to unsafe sites. Here, too, your goal is to block as many "bad" pop-ups as possible while allowing legitimate ones to get through the barriers.

To work with these settings, open Internet Explorer, click **Tools**, and then click **Internet Options**. Click the Privacy tab to display the dialog box shown in Figure 6.

Figure 6   *Make this your starting point to adjust settings for how Internet Explorer handles cookies and pop-up windows.*

The slider control under the **Settings** heading in this dialog box lets you choose one of six predefined groups of settings that dictate how Internet Explorer will respond when you visit a site that wants to create a cookie on your computer. Slide the control up to add extra privacy protection, or slide it down to relax the protection.

If you're not all that concerned about privacy, you can leave this setting at Medium, and you won't be bothered by any further dialog boxes. However, I prefer a more active control over cookies. Whenever I visit a site for the first time, I want to decide whether that site should be allowed to create a cookie, and after I make that decision I don't want to be bothered again when I return to that site. Likewise, I want to block *all* third-party cookies, which are typically used by advertising firms to track my movements across different Web sites on their network. To use the same settings that I do, follow these steps:

1   Click **Advanced**. This opens the Advanced Privacy Settings dialog box.

2   Adjust the settings so that they match those shown here:

- Click to select the check box to the left of **Override automatic cookie handling**.

- Under **First-party Cookies**, click **Prompt**. Under **Third-party Cookies**, click **Block**.

- Click to select the check box to the left of **Always allow session cookies**.

3   Click **OK** to save your changes.

From now on, whenever you visit a Web site for the first time, you'll see a Privacy Alert dialog box like the one shown below. To set your preference for all pages from that site, click the check box to the left of **Apply my decision to all cookies from this Web site** and then click **Allow Cookie** if you trust the site or **Block Cookie** if you want to ban all cookies from that site.

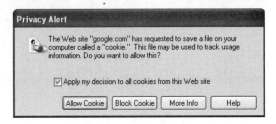

To control the way Internet Explorer handles pop-ups, return to the Internet Options dialog box, click the Privacy tab, and adjust the settings under the **Pop-up Blocker** heading. If you prefer to use another pop-up-blocking program, you should disable the pop-up blocker here by clearing the check box to the left of **Block pop-ups**.

TIP   If you inadvertently block a site that you actually meant to trust, or vice versa, open the Internet Options dialog box again, click the Privacy tab, and click Sites. Click the name of the site you accidentally added to the list and then click Remove. Click OK to return to Internet Explorer, and reload any page from that site to see a fresh Privacy Alert prompt.

For more control over which pop-ups get blocked, click **Settings**. The Pop-up Blocker Settings dialog box, shown below, allows you to adjust the following options:

- **Sounds.**   Normally, Windows plays a sound every time a pop-up is blocked. If you find the sound effects annoying, clear the **Play a sound when a pop-up is blocked** check box.

- **Information Bar.**   When a pop-up is blocked, the Information Bar, which will appear just below the Address bar in your browser window, alerts you to this fact. I recommend that you leave the box to the left of **Show Information Bar when a pop-up is blocked** selected. If you hide this bar, you'll find it difficult to enable a "good" pop-up that inadvertently gets blocked.

- **Filter level.**   The list at the bottom of the dialog box lets you choose a Low, Medium, or High setting for the pop-up blocker. I recommend that you leave this setting at the default: **Medium: Block most automatic pop-ups**.

You've now completed the essential precautions to make sure your computer is well protected from common security risks. Your next step is to get connected to other computers around you. Even if you don't plan to create your own local area network, I recommend you read the next chapter to learn how to connect your new PC to your old one so that you can quickly and efficiently transfer your files and settings later.

Step 3: **Get Connected**

You have an old PC. You have a new PC. You might even have a few other computers in your home or small business. That means you're already well on the way to having your own local area network.

Thanks to Microsoft Windows XP, you no longer need an engineering degree to set up a network. With inexpensive, off-the-shelf hardware and the help of a few wizards, in fact, you should have your network up and running in less than an hour. When you do, you'll be able to share a single high-speed Internet connection, copy files and folders between computers, print documents on a shared printer connected to another computer, and play games using multiple computers. You'll also find that using a network is the fastest, easiest way to transfer files and computer settings to your new PC.

To get the most out of a Windows XP–based network, it helps to understand the basic principles of Windows networking. That's especially true if you need to troubleshoot problems with a network. But you don't need any specialized knowledge to accomplish the tasks in this chapter. I explain everything you need to do to set up a secure, functional network in a home or small business.

☑ Checklist:

☐ **Assemble your network hardware (page 86).** Every computer on your network needs its own network adapter (wired or wireless). You also need a router with an integrated switch or hub to tie the pieces together. If any of your adapters are wireless, the router needs to include a wireless access point as well.

☐ **Set up wired network connections (page 89).** Windows Plug and Play installs the proper drivers for you. Most of the configuration is automatic as well, thanks to the Network Setup Wizard.

☐ **Set up wireless network connections (page 95).** Be sure to set up encryption on your wireless access point and write down the network key. Enter the key when prompted by Windows, and you're ready to connect.

☐ **Set up additional network computers (page 98).** The Network Setup Wizard handles this chore for any computer running a recent version of Windows.

☐ **Share files and folders (page 99).** Windows XP sets up a Shared Documents folder for you, where you can save files you want to share over the network. You can also share other folders.

☐ **Create shortcuts to shared files on other computers (page 104).** For easier access, drag icons from the My Network Places folder and drop them on the desktop, on the Start menu, or in the My Documents folder.

☐ **Test and troubleshoot (page 105).** Make sure everything's working the way it should.

Assemble your network hardware

Before your computers can communicate with one another, you need to add the right hardware. Here's a list of all the pieces you'll require:

- **Router with integrated switch or hub.** Sometimes called a residential gateway, this small box is the central distribution point of your network. Your high-speed modem plugs into the Wide Area Network (WAN) port, and each computer with a wired network adapter plugs into one of the Local Area Network (LAN) ports. Although you can purchase a hub or switch that doesn't include a router, I strongly recommend that you choose one of the many devices that combine both functions in a single box.

- **Network adapters.** These devices manage communications between a PC and a network. You'll need one for each PC on your network. Most new desktop computers include a wired network adapter, which can be connected directly to a router using a standard patch cable. Portable PCs might include a wired adapter, a wireless adapter, or both. If your computer doesn't include a network adapter, you can add an inexpensive internal card using an open PCI slot or purchase a network adapter that plugs into the universal serial bus (USB) port instead. With portable computers, you can also use a network adapter in the PC card format (technically known as PCMCIA), which plugs into the credit card–sized slots on most notebook computers.

  TIP   Although wireless network adapters are most commonly found in notebook computers, they can also be used in desktop computers. To add a wireless adapter to an existing desktop computer, choose an internal device in the standard PCI format, which installs in an empty expansion slot inside your PC, or get an external device that plugs into an external USB port.

- **Wireless access point.** This component is necessary if you plan to use any wireless adapters on your network. The simplest and most cost-effective way to add wireless capabilities to your network is to choose a router that includes an integrated wireless access point.

- **Network cables.** To connect each wired adapter to your router, you'll use unshielded twisted-pair (UTP) Category 5 cabling, which consists of eight individual color-coded strands of wire (four pairs) terminated by an RJ-45 connector on either end. If that description is too complicated, just visit any well-stocked computer store and ask where they keep the patch cables. You'll find patch cables in a variety of lengths; make sure each cable is long enough for the physical layout of computers on your network.

Figure 1 shows how you connect the pieces of a typical network with a broadband connection and a mix of wired and wireless network adapters.

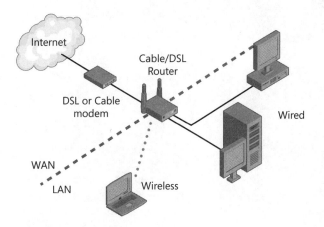

Figure 1   *A secure Windows XP network includes a router and can accommodate PCs with a mix of wired and wireless adapters.*

Should you use wired or wireless adapters? That depends on the physical layout of your home or office. If you're planning to connect two computers that are side by side in your home office, you can plug both computers directly into a router, using two short patch cables. On the other hand, if your kids have a PC upstairs and your new PC is in a downstairs office, you'll probably want to mix wireless and wired adapters. In that case, choose a router that also includes a wireless access point and connect it to the high-speed Internet connection in your office. Add a wireless adapter to the upstairs computer and run through the appropriate wizards, and your network is complete. Just be certain that all the hardware you select is compatible with Windows XP.

TIP   If you want to connect two computers directly, without using a hub, switch, or router, you can do so by plugging a *crossover cable* into the RJ-45 port on each computer's network adapter. Although a crossover cable looks exactly like a standard network patch cable, the internal wiring is slightly different, with the connections on one pair of wires reversed. Using a crossover cable is not practical as a long-term networking solution; it is, however, an ideal way to transfer data to your new PC if you don't want or need a permanent network.

Why You Need a Router

Do you want to add an extra layer of security to your network? Get a router and use its firewall features in conjunction with the software-based Windows Firewall—the combination is hard to beat. Here's why.

Every computer that uses the TCP/IP protocol has a unique *IP address*: a numeric ID that identifies the source and destination of data packets as they move around. When you connect directly to the Internet (by connecting your PC to a cable modem, for instance), you get a public IP address that's visible to anyone. That includes hackers, who scan public IP addresses looking for PCs with security holes. If they find one, they can break in and do untold damage.

By connecting a router to your cable modem and plugging your computer into the router's LAN ports, you effectively hide your PC. Your ISP assigns a public IP address to the router, and the router in turn supplies private IP addresses to the computers on your network. Every incoming and outgoing packet of data goes through the router, which passes data to your computer only when it confirms that you specifically requested that data. If an outside computer tries to make an unsolicited connection to the public IP address on your router, it gets swatted away.

A router is a great addition to a network of any size. In fact, you can use its protection even if you have a single computer!

In this chapter, I assume your new PC has a network adapter (wired or wireless) with the correct drivers installed, that you have already installed a router and set up your Internet connection (see page 59), and that you have installed network adapters and any required drivers in other computers on your network.

CAUTION Are the other computers on your network running older versions of Windows? If that's the case, you may find a few more headaches. Later in this chapter, I'll explain how to access shared files and printers on computers running other versions of Windows, and how to access shared resources on your new PC from those older computers, but you're on your own when it comes to getting those older PCs set up initially. For best results, I recommend you upgrade those computers to Windows XP if possible.

Set up wired network connections

If you have a high-speed Internet connection, you already did the lion's share of the work of configuring your new PC for network access in the previous chapter. If you have only a dial-up network connection, or if you skipped over any steps for setting up a network earlier, you can rerun the Network Setup Wizard now. Doing so configures the Windows networking components so that computers on the network can communicate with one another. It also enables or disables file and printer sharing, configures the Windows Firewall for your network type, and sets attributes on shared folders that allow access to those folders from other computers on the network.

At this point, you can also connect any other computers on your network that have wired connections and are running Windows XP. Plug in one end of a patch cable to the network adapter's RJ-45 port and then connect the other end to a LAN port on the router. When you've finished this process for each computer on the network, run the Network Setup Wizard.

Click **Start**, click **Control Panel**, and then click **Network and Internet Connections**. (If this option isn't available, click **Switch to Category View**, under the **Control Panel** heading on the left side of the window.) Under the **Pick a Task** heading, click **Set up or change your home or small office network**. The Network Setup Wizard opens.

NOTE To set up any network components, you must be logged on as a member of the Administrators group. If you're the owner of the computer, this should be no problem. If your user account is set up as a Limited user, you'll need to switch to an Administrator account to proceed.

Click **Next** to page through the wizard's steps, following its prompts; the exact steps will vary slightly, depending on your network configuration:

- **Broadband network with router.** If you followed the steps in the previous chapter in the "Set up a high-speed Internet connection" section (page 59), your PC should be correctly set up. If you chose not to enable file and printer sharing at that time, run through the wizard again. On the **Do you want to use the shared connection?** page, click **Yes, use the existing shared Internet connection for this computer's Internet access (recommended)**.

If the wizard doesn't detect your router, you'll reach the **Select a connection method** dialog box, where you should click **This computer connects to the Internet through a residential gateway or through another computer on my network**. On the **File and printer sharing** page, click **Turn on file and printer sharing**. Do the same for any other computer running Windows XP on your network.

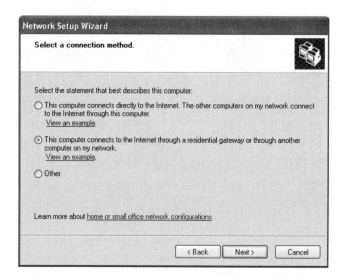

- **Direct connection with crossover cable.** Use this option to establish a temporary network connection for transferring files between two computers. After you connect both computers using a crossover cable (a standard patch cable will not work), run the Network Setup Wizard, click **Other** on the **Select a connection method** dialog box, and then click **This computer belongs to a network that does not have an Internet connection.** Windows displays the **Limited or no connectivity** warning in the status dialog box shown here. You can safely ignore this message.

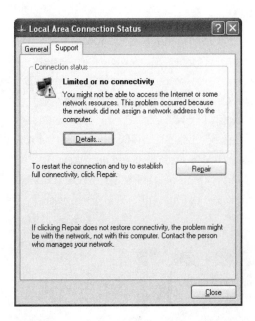

When you reach the **File and printer sharing** page, be sure to click the **Turn on file and printer sharing** option. Finish the wizard and create a Network Setup disk (or use the Windows XP CD) to configure the other computer. After you run the wizard on the other PC, your two-PC network should be up and running.

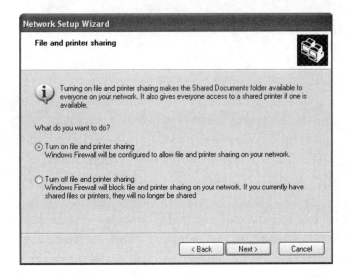

● **Unshared dial-up Internet connection with a wired network.** Does your computer include a network adapter, a modem, and no broadband connection? In this configuration, you can choose to use dial-up Internet access on your own computer and set up a network to share files separately with other computers. Run the Network Setup Wizard and click **Other** on the **Select a connection method** dialog box. Click **Next** to advance to the **Other Internet connection methods...** page and click the check box to the left of **This computer belongs to a network that does not have an Internet connection.** On the **File and printer sharing** page, click the **Turn on file and printer sharing** option. Finish the wizard, creating a network setup disk if needed.

● **Shared dial-up Internet connection with a wired network.** If your computer includes a network adapter and a modem, with no broadband connection, you can allow other computers on your network to share your dial-up Internet connection. With Internet Connection Sharing (ICS) enabled, other computers on your network can access the Internet without a modem or a direct connection of their own, by passing data through your computer. To set up ICS, run the Network Setup Wizard and click **This computer connects directly to the Internet. Other computers on my network connect to the Internet through this computer** on the **Select a connection method** dialog box.

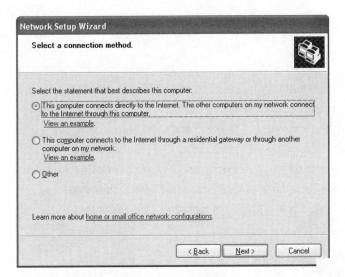

Click **Next** to advance to the **Select your Internet connection** page. The wizard displays a list of all available Internet connections; click to select your default Internet connection, which should already be highlighted, and then click **Next**.

NOTE This procedure assumes that you have already set up your dial-up connection using the steps outlined in "Configure a dial-up Internet connection," beginning on page 63.

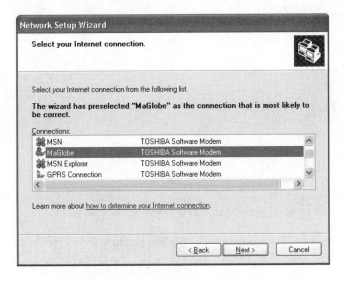

On the **File and printer sharing** page, click the **Turn on file and printer sharing** option. Finish the wizard, creating a network setup disk if needed.

When you enable Internet Connection Sharing, the wizard turns on automatic dialing and also grants users of other computers the capability to disconnect the dial-up connection on your computer. Of course, your computer must be turned on for ICS to work. You can change these settings so that other people can access the shared Internet connection only when you choose to dial up. To do so, open Control Panel and click **Network and Internet Connections**. Click **Network Connections** to open the folder containing your dial-up connections. Right-click the shared connection, click **Properties**, and click the Advanced tab. Figure 2 shows the resulting dialog box.

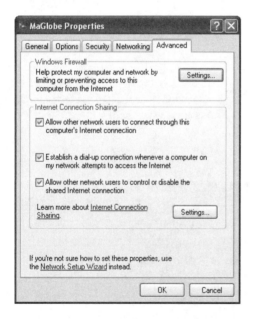

Figure 2   *If you use Internet Connection Sharing, control its settings from this dialog box.*

The three check boxes under the **Internet Connection Sharing** heading control how the service works. Normally, all three are selected when ICS is enabled.

● **Allow other network users to connect through this computer's Internet connection** is the ICS "on/off" switch. Clear this box to disable ICS completely.

- **Establish a dial-up connection whenever a computer on my network attempts to access the Internet** controls automatic dialing. If you clear this box, you will be able to connect to the Internet or disconnect, but other computers will get an error message if they try to browse the Web or check e-mail when you're disconnected.

- **Allow other network users to control or disable the shared Internet connection** shows or hides a control icon on other computers. Using this icon, which is found in the My Network Places folder, someone using another computer can dial or hang up your Internet connection manually. Clear the check box to disable this function.

CAUTION Internet Connection Sharing works with broadband connections as well. You need two network adapters in your computer—one for your network and one for your high-speed Internet connection. In effect, this turns your computer into a router. I don't recommend this setup. A dedicated router, which is specifically built for the purpose, provides more effective control over a shared Internet connection.

☐ Set up wireless network connections

A few years ago, wireless networking was exotic, technically complex, and very expensive. Today, you can choose from a wide range of inexpensive wireless networking products, and setup is simple if you use the new Wireless Network Setup Wizard introduced in Windows SP2. Before you can get your wireless connection working, you need to do the following:

1 **Set up your wireless access point.** Every hardware design is different, so you'll need to check the manual that came with your access point. Most such devices use a Web browser as the interface for setup purposes; you type in a standard address to connect to the access point and enable its configuration interface. If your network combines wired and wireless devices, use a wired computer to do this initial setup.

TIP If you have a Linksys router, the default address to access the administrative interface is *http://192.168.1.1*; leave the user name blank and use the password **admin**. SMC routers use *http://192.168.2.1* as the default address, with a blank user name and password. If you have a Netgear router, the default address is *http://192.168.0.1*; the default user name is **admin** and the password is **password**. As part of the setup process, be sure to change the user name and password from these not-so-secure defaults!

2 **Make a note of the Service Set Identifier (SSID) of your access point.** The SSID is the name that identifies your wireless network. Every access point supplies a default name. ("Default" and "wireless" are common, as are manufacturers' names such as "linksys" and "netgear.") Using the administrative interface, you can change the default SSID to something that is more descriptive of your network, but this step isn't necessary.

3 **Choose an encryption method.** Anyone who comes within range of your access point can connect to it. Once connected, they can use your Internet connection and peek through any shared files and folders on your network. If you live in an apartment building or have neighbors within a few hundred feet, or if your access point is in an office, this is a genuine security risk. But even if you think you're

CAUTION Although it's possible to set up a so-called open wireless connection, with no encryption at all, I do not recommend that you do so. An open wireless connection offers an open invitation to hackers to break in, and some people have actually turned wireless hacking into a sport. Setting up encryption is simple, and the results are quite effective. Don't skip this step!

safe, I recommend you enable encryption on your access point. You'll have no trouble connecting, but unauthorized users will be locked out. Your choices, which I explain in more detail in a few moments, include Wi-Fi Protected Access (WPA) and Wired Equivalent Privacy (WEP). Choose WPA if your access point and adapter support it; if either piece of hardware is incompatible with WPA, use WEP instead.

4 **Write down your network key.** When you enable encryption, every bit of data you send around on your wireless network is encrypted so that it can't be intercepted by anyone else. To properly encrypt and decrypt this data, every piece of your wireless network must use a matching key, which is a string of numbers and letters. Every access point has a different method of setting this key. One popular technique is to have you enter a pass phrase (such as "I wish to complain about this parrot" or "It was the best of times, it was the worst of times"), which is then used to generate a key. You enter the key into the configuration dialog box for your wireless adapter, and everything works as it should.

5 **Install drivers for your wireless adapter.** This should be done automatically as part of Windows Plug and Play. If you're adding an adapter to an existing computer, you may need to supply a driver CD to complete the installation.

In this section, I assume that you are using Windows XP to manage your wireless connection. Some wireless devices include their own custom utility software designed to help manage the device. In general, these utilities were designed for older versions of Windows and you should disable them with Windows XP.

When you turn on a PC equipped with a wireless network adapter, Windows automatically scans for available wireless access points. When it finds your wireless access point, it pops up a balloon message in the notification area in the lower right corner of your display:

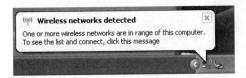

Click the balloon to open a list of available networks, as shown in Figure 3. If you've set your wireless access point correctly, the SSID of your access point should appear here. The green bars at the right indicate the strength of the wireless signal. If you enabled WEP or WPA, you'll see the padlock icon shown here, next to the **Security-enabled wireless network** label.

TIP   If the balloon message disappears before you can click it, right-click the Wireless Network Connection icon in the notification area and then click View Available Networks on the shortcut menu.

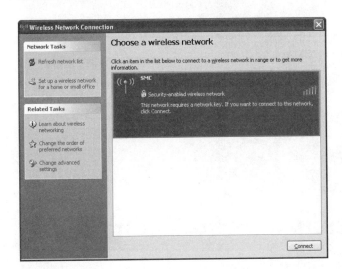

Figure 3   *Click Connect to enable communication between your PC and the selected wireless access point. Because this network is secure, you'll need to enter a network key.*

Wireless Networks Made Easy

If you have a brand-new wireless access point specifically designed for Windows XP, you may be able to use the new Wireless Network Setup Wizard to configure your access point and your network card for maximum security without having to type a single character. Using the wizard, you can automatically create a super-strong WPA key, assign it to your wireless network adapter, and copy the settings to your access point using a USB flash key.

To get started, open Control Panel, click **Network and Internet Connections**, and click **Wireless Network Setup Wizard**. Follow the wizard's prompts to set up your network. When you're done, the wizard prompts you to insert a flash drive and copy the setting. Remove the flash drive from the PC, plug it into the USB port on your wireless access point, and configuration is complete.

As I write this book, no wireless equipment manufacturers offer routers that support this feature, and none are on the horizon. In this chapter, I therefore assume you're setting things up the old-fashioned way.

When you click **Connect**, Windows opens a dialog box that allows you to enter the network key. This key is not case-sensitive. If you're using WEP, the key will consist of five characters (for 40-bit encryption) or 13 characters (104-bit encryption). If you're using WPA, the key can be up to 26 characters long.

TIP When entering a network key, every character counts. If you're having trouble connecting, check the key on your access point again. Pay special attention to letters and numbers that can be confused, such as the letter O and the number 0.

After you enter the key, click **Connect**. If the key you entered matches the one used on the access point, Windows makes the connection, and the display changes to reflect your active status.

Set up additional network computers

After you set up your PC, finish the task of setting up your network by configuring each computer that's a part of your network. If those computers are running any modern version of Windows—including Windows 98, Windows Millennium Edition (Windows Me), or Windows XP—all you need to do is run the Network Setup

Wizard. To do so, insert the Windows XP CD in the CD-ROM drive of the other computer, click **Perform additional tasks** on the **Welcome to Microsoft Windows XP** page, and then click **Set up a home or small office network**.

When you run the Network Setup Wizard on other computers, it performs the exact same tasks as on your new PC. (On computers running Windows 98 or Windows Me, you may need to restart the computer once at the beginning of the wizard and again at the end to complete the setup process.) When you finish running the wizard on all other computers that are a part of your network, move on to the next step.

TIP   If the Windows XP CD is unavailable, you can create a Network Setup disk as the final step of the Network Setup Wizard. Have a blank, formatted floppy disk or USB flash drive handy. This step of the wizard adds a file called Netsetup.exe to the target disk. Insert that disk in the other computer, open My Computer, double-click the icon for the drive that contains the Network Setup Wizard files, and then double-click Netsetup.

Share files and folders

The primary purpose of setting up a network is to allow people to share files and folders. (You can also access shared printers on a network, but we'll wait to do that until we get to "Set up and share a printer," which begins on page 147.)

When you run the Network Setup Wizard and enable file sharing, you automatically make the Shared Documents folder and its contents available over the network. In addition, you can choose to make files in other locations available to network users. File sharing works in the opposite direction as well—with the right preparation, you can access shared folders on other computers.

NOTE   When I talk of file sharing in this chapter, I'm referring exclusively to sharing over a small network that is not part of a Windows domain. I assume that you're using the Simple File Sharing feature that is used in Windows XP Home Edition. This setting is also the default setting in Windows XP Professional, although if you use this operating system you can switch to the more complicated Classic File Sharing feature. Explaining the ins and outs of Classic File Sharing would take another book the size of this one. If you're really interested, pick up a copy of *Microsoft Windows XP Inside Out, Second Edition*, by Ed Bott, Carl Siechert, and Craig Stinson (Microsoft Press, 2004).

Before you share any files on your network, let's run through the ins and outs of file sharing:

- All files and folders in your Shared Documents folder are automatically available for anyone on your network to access. You cannot add a password to protect files in this location.

- For each shared folder, you can specify whether you want other people to have read-only access to those files or also have the ability to change files. If you choose the latter option, there are no restrictions on the capability of other people to view, edit, or delete files stored here or in subfolders in this location.

- All files in the Shared Documents folder on other networked computers running Windows XP are available to you, providing that file sharing is enabled on those computers.

- When you use the Network Setup Wizard to enable file sharing, it configures the Windows Firewall so that computers on your network can access shared files but computers elsewhere (on the Internet, in particular) are blocked from shared folders.

- If you chose the option to make your personal files private—see "Add a password to your user account," page 50—you cannot share the files in your My Documents folder or any of its subfolders.

- You can't share individual files, only folders. When you share a folder over the network, all files within that folder, as well as all files in subfolders in that location, are available to others.

- If other computers on your network are running Windows 98 or Windows Me, shared folders on those computers can be protected with a password. Windows XP prompts you to enter this password when you access those shared folders. You can save this password so that you don't have to continually enter it.

Every computer has a unique name, and every shared folder has a name that identifies the share. The share name does not have to be the same as the name of the folder it points to. Together, these two names allow you to gain access to shared folders on your network.

NOTE The share name of the Shared Documents folder on any computer running Windows XP is SharedDocs.

To connect directly to a shared folder, click **Start** and then click **Run**. In the Run box, enter two backslashes (\\), followed by the computer name, a single backslash, and the share name. For instance, if your computer is named Bianca, you can connect to your Shared Documents folder from another computer on the network by typing \\bianca\shareddocs in the Run box. (Don't worry about capital letters—computer and share names are not case-sensitive.)

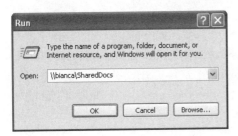

To see all the shared folders available on your network, click **Start** and then click **My Network Places**. The icons in the **Local Network** category show the share name, the description of the computer (if available), and the computer name. Figure 4 shows what this folder looks like on a medium-sized network.

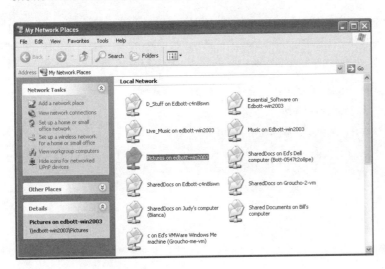

Figure 4   *Every shared folder on every computer on your network shows up here, in the My Network Places folder. Double-click an icon to open that folder.*

If you look inside the Shared Documents folder, you'll find subfolders for Shared Music and Shared Pictures. To share digital music and picture files with other people on your network, drag the files out of the My Pictures and My Music folders (where they're available only to you) and drop them here, in these shared folders:

 Shared Music   Shared Pictures

When should you share other folders? On my computer, I have a very large collection of digital music that I keep on its own dedicated hard disk, in a folder called Live Music. I share the contents of that hard drive so that other people on the network can listen to tunes from that collection on their computers, too. If you have similar folders that you want to share, follow these steps:

1 Open Windows Explorer, right-click the icon of the folder you want to share, and click **Sharing and Security**. This opens a Properties dialog box for the selected folder and displays the Sharing tab.

2 Click to select the check box to the left of **Share the folder on the network**.

3 In the **Share name** box, Windows automatically fills in the name of the folder. Change this name if you want.

TIP   I recommend that you replace any spaces with underlines and keep the total length of the name to 12 characters or fewer; this allows computers running older versions of Windows to access the shared files.

4 If you want other people to be able to add, edit, or delete files in this location, click the check box to the left of **Allow network users to change my files**.

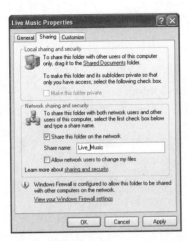

5 Click OK to save your changes.

When you return to Windows Explorer, you'll see that the folder icon now has a hand under it, indicating that the folder is available for access over the network:

You can have as many shared folders as you want on a computer. If you try to share an entire drive by clicking the drive-letter icon in My Computer, Windows will warn you that you could be risking security problems. I recommend that you follow this advice and avoid sharing the root folder of a hard disk drive. Instead, create a subfolder on the drive, store the files you want to share in that subfolder, and then share the subfolder.

Create shortcuts to shared files on other computers

The simplest way to access shared folders on other computers is to click **Start**, click **My Network Places**, and double-click the icon that represents the shared folder.

That might represent more steps than you want to go through, however, especially for folders you use frequently. To make any shared folder more easily accessible, drag its icon from the My Network Places folder and drop it on the desktop, on the Start button, or in the My Documents folder. Doing so creates a shortcut to the shared folder.

In the case of password-protected folders on a network computer running Windows 98 or Windows Me, you may find that double-clicking the icon of the shared folder (or manually entering the computer name and share name in the correct format) results in a dialog box that prompts you for the password. (The user name is unavailable, because Windows XP always logs on to network computers using the Guest account.)

Enter the password here. If you click the box to the left of **Remember my password**, Windows stores your password as part of your user account. If you don't store the password, you have to type it the first time you access the shared folder in each session.

Test and troubleshoot

If you've performed all the steps in this chapter so far, you should have a functioning network. Now is the time to test the connection from each computer and make sure everything is working properly.

For starters, look in the My Network Places folder and verify that you can see icons for all the shared folders on your network. Double-click each icon to open the shared folder and make sure it works.

If you have trouble opening any folder or if you don't see any icons in My Network Places, here are some troubleshooting steps to try.

Open Control Panel, click **Network and Internet Connections**, and click **Network Connections**. Double-click the Local Area Connection icon. The information in the status dialog box tells you whether you have a proper connection.

- On the General tab, you can see the speed of the connection and you can watch any current activity.

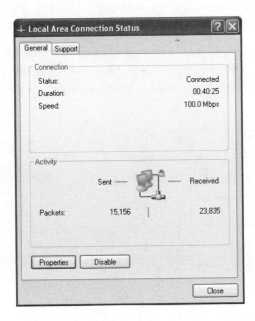

● Click the Support tab to see technical information about your connection.\

If you're having trouble connecting to another machine on your network, make sure both machines are on the same subnet—that is, they have IP address numbers that are in the same range. For instance, the IP address of the computer shown above is 192.168.2.100. If you check the IP address on another computer on your network and its address is 169.254.101.50, the two computers are on different subnets and will be unable to communicate.

To fix the problem, click the Repair button on the Status tab. This resets most network configuration details and will often fix a simple problem. If this option doesn't work, try running the Network Setup Wizard again on both connections, making sure to specify the same workgroup name.

If you're unable to connect to a shared folder on another computer, make sure the folder is shared properly. Right-click the folder icon, click **Sharing and Security**, and check to see that the **Share this folder on the network** box is selected.

Don't overlook the Windows Firewall as a source of problems. If you used the Network Setup Wizard, this setting should be OK, but it's worth checking anyway:

1 Click **Start**, click **Control Panel**, and click **Security Center**.

2 At the bottom of the Security Center dialog box, click **Windows Firewall**.

3 Click the Exceptions tab, and verify that the box to the left of **File and Printer Sharing** in the **Programs and Services** list is selected.

If all else fails, try the Network Troubleshooter. Open Control Panel, and click **Network and Internet Connections**. In the task pane on the left, under the **Troubleshooters** heading, click **Home or Small Office Networking**. Follow the meticulous Q&A to see if you can identify the problem.

Step 4: **Move Files and Settings**

How long have you been using your old PC? Most people hang on to a computer for three to five years, long enough to build up a huge collection of documents, spreadsheets, databases, digital pictures, downloaded music, and other data files, not to mention plenty of passwords, hundreds of e-mail messages, and a bulging address book. During that time, you've also customized the way Microsoft Windows works and tweaked the preferences of each program so that it works the way you do.

All those files and settings are on your old computer. How do you move them to your new PC? Unfortunately, there's no magic wand that will automatically transfer everything in the twinkling of an eye, but you do have options.

In this chapter, I'll explain those options and help you pick the best approach for your situation. My personal recommendation—and the one I'll spend the most time on in this chapter—is using the Windows XP Files and Settings Transfer Wizard. It's not perfect, and it's certainly not easy to use, but it does a surprisingly good job of moving what really matters onto your old PC and putting it in a logical place.

☑ Checklist:

❑ **Choose a file-transfer option (page 110).** I recommend using the Files and Settings Transfer Wizard over a network. But you have other options as well.

❑ **Prepare for the move (page 112).** Organize your data files first and you'll have an easier time later.

❑ **Back up important files and settings (page 114).** If you choose not to use the wizard, you can use these techniques to export e-mail and data files to your new PC.

❑ **Choose your transfer method (page 117).** If you have a local area network, this is your best option. You can also use a removable hard drive or a USB flash key.

❑ **Customize your transfer options (page 121).** The Files and Settings Transfer Wizard lets you specify exactly what you want to transfer to your new PC.

❑ **Make the move (page 125).** Follow the wizard's prompts and avoid a few common gotchas.

❑ **Test and troubleshoot (page 127).** Don't delete the files from your old computer until you're sure that everything transferred correctly to the new one.

❑ Choose a file-transfer option

The task of moving files and settings can be incredibly simple, or it can turn into a major production that lasts for hours. Before you invest a lot of time and energy in this task, think about how much data you have and whether you really want to move all of it your new PC. These are your options:

- **Copy your files using removable media.** If you have a small number of files and they don't occupy a lot of space, you can copy them to removable media (floppy disks, Zip disks, or CDs you burn with a CD-R drive) and then copy the contents of those disks onto your new PC. This option will not copy any of your program settings, nor will it export your e-mail messages or address book.

- **Copy files over a network.** This option is similar to the previous one, only simpler. If all your files are in one location and you have set up a network connection, you can open Windows Explorer on your old computer, connect to the Shared Documents folder on your new PC, and begin copying files. After you've moved the files, you can reorganize them on the new PC.

> **CAUTION** If you use Outlook Express as your e-mail program, you cannot directly copy your messages and address book to your new PC. You *must* use either the Files and Settings Transfer Wizard or a third-party utility to export your e-mail. Keep reading.

- **Export selected files and settings.** Some programs offer an option to export settings and data files, either through a menu choice on the program itself or with the help of an external utility. This option is especially appropriate for e-mail programs and Web browsers. If you use Microsoft Outlook (a part of Microsoft Office) or Outlook Express as your e-mail program, for instance, you can choose several free utilities that handle this chore. (I list these options in detail later in this chapter, under the heading "Back up your most important files," page 114.)

- **Use a backup program.** If you've been using a dedicated backup program to save copies of your data files, you can install that program on your new PC and restore the backed-up files. This is an effective way to move files between computers, but it doesn't do much for settings and it may or may not move your e-mail messages and address book. If you've been using ⌐ backup program and you're comfortable with its operation, go ahead and use it.

● **Use third-party file transfer software.** Several companies make commercial programs that promise to transfer your files, settings, and even your programs to your new PC. Most of these programs are designed for use in large corporations, where computer professionals are responsible for setting up hundreds of new computers every year. I've looked at these programs and don't recommend any of them for the tasks discussed in this chapter.

● **Use the Files and Settings Transfer Wizard.** This free utility is included with all versions of Windows XP. You can use it to transfer all of your data files, most custom Windows settings (such as your desktop colors, fonts, and wallpaper), and preferences for some programs to your new PC. In the remainder of this section, I focus on the pros and cons of this tool.

Here, in a nutshell, is how the Files and Settings Transfer Wizard works and how you work with it:

● First, you organize your files and make certain you've accounted for everything you want to transfer.

● Next, you decide how you want to transfer the files. The best options are to transfer everything directly over a network or to use an external hard disk or flash key as an intermediate storage location. If you choose to use a local area network or a direct cable connection, you run the wizard on the new computer first. If you're using any other method, you start with the old PC first.

● You run the wizard on your old PC. It looks in your My Documents folder and on your desktop (and in a few other locations). It also searches your entire hard disk for any files that appear to be data files, regardless of where they're stored. Finally, it goes through the Registry and collects your customized settings for Windows and for certain other programs. If you prefer, you can specify that you only want certain types of settings and files to be transferred. You can also tell the wizard to search for files stored in specific locations only.

● After the wizard scans your hard disk, it makes a list of all the settings and files you chose and gathers the contents of that list for transferring. You can make the transfer directly, over a network, or save the files to an intermediate location such as a shared network folder.

- On the new PC, the wizard puts the transferred files in a location that matches where they were on the old PC. It adds custom settings, where it finds them, to the Windows Registry.

NOTE You can reinstall your software before or after running the wizard. In a very small number of instances (with WinZip and Adobe Reader, for instance), you need to install the program on the new computer first for the settings to be successfully transferred. The Files and Settings Transfer Wizard warns you if any of the installed programs on your old computer are in this category.

Sounds great so far, right? So, what's the catch?

The wizard's biggest drawback is what it doesn't do. It doesn't transfer your installed programs to your new PC. For that, you have to reinstall everything—a task we'll tackle together in "Step 6: Instant Productivity: Just Add Software," beginning on page 152. For security reasons, it doesn't transfer any passwords that are saved on your old computer, except for some Web page logon information stored in browser cookies.

And the wizard might transfer more than you want, especially if you have old files created by programs you no longer use. If you have a large collection of digital music, pictures, or video, the transfer can take a long, long time.

If you understand those limitations and you decide you want to use the Files and Settings Transfer Wizard, keep going through this entire chapter. I'll show you, in detail, how to make the wizard work for you. If you choose another method for transferring files and settings, at least read the next two sections, "Prepare for the move" and "Back up your most important files." Both of these sections include suggestions for things you can do to make this process easier.

Prepare for the move

Remember at the beginning of this book, when you put together a list of all the programs installed on your old computer that you want to transfer to your new PC. (If you skipped this step, it's not too late—go back to "Gather your program disks," page 8, and follow the instructions there.) Go through that list of programs, make a note of the types of data files each one uses, and then locate the data files those programs use. The easiest way to do this is to open the program on your old computer and try to open an existing file. In the Open dialog box, make a note of the folder where these files are stored.

If you've been diligent and the program follows Windows standards, your data files should be in the My Documents folder, or one of its subfolders. Not all programs are so well behaved, however. Some older programs in particular may steer you into storing your data files in odd locations, such as a folder in the same location where the program files are located. If you find any files in inappropriate locations, move them into the My Documents folder—creating a new subfolder, if necessary—so that you are more easily able to locate them later.

TIP   This is a great time to clean house, as long as you don't get bogged down in the process. If you find you have lots of files you no longer need, delete them. If you need to keep copies but don't need quick access, archive them using a more appropriate storage medium, such as a CD or DVD. If you have digital pictures and music files scattered around your hard disk, move those files into My Pictures and My Music, respectively.

Table 1 shows the names of folders that are automatically copied in their entirety. In addition, the wizard looks for files whose extensions match a long list of file types; it copies those files even if they're located outside one of the standard folders shown here.

Table 1: Common Data Folders

Folder Name	What's Stored There...
My Documents	Your personal documents, including the contents of My Music, My Videos, and other subfolders, but not My Pictures.
My Pictures	All your digital pictures. Although this is a subfolder of My Documents, the wizard treats it separately.
Desktop	All the junk on your desktop, including program shortcuts, downloaded files, and stuff you stopped using ages ago.
Quick Launch	Program icons from the Quick Launch toolbar.
Fonts	All your Windows standard fonts, plus any custom fonts you've added and fonts installed along with a program you installed.
Shared Desktop	Shortcuts created when you install a new program. The contents of this folder are visible to anyone who logs on to the computer.
Shared Documents	Files that are available to other people who log on to your computer or connect to the computer over your local network.

Back up important files and settings

Strictly speaking, this step isn't necessary. Using the Files and Settings Transfer Wizard doesn't change or delete any existing files on your old PC, so if anything goes wrong with the transfer you haven't lost any data. However, you might decide after looking at the steps here that you want to use this method to transfer some types of information, especially for programs that don't use the Files and Settings Transfer Wizard. If you have any programs that offer the option to export data to a new computer, take advantage of that feature. Here are some tips on how to back up and restore common types of data:

● **Internet Explorer Favorites.** The Files and Settings Transfer Wizard copies all your favorites as part of its default settings. To back up your Favorites into a simple text file, open Internet Explorer, click **File**, and then click **Import and Export**. Follow the wizard's prompts, choosing the **Export Favorites** option on the **Import/Export Selection** page.

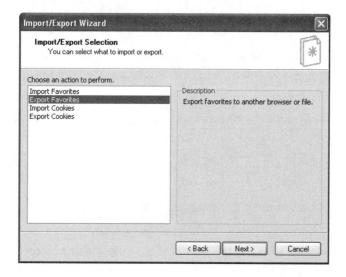

On the **Export Favorites Source Folder** page, select the Favorites folder at the top level of the list. On the **Export Favorites Destination** page, click **Browse** and choose a folder. (I create a new folder in My Documents called My Backup Files.) Click **Finish** to save the file. To copy the saved Favorites to your new PC, copy the file to a floppy disk, a USB flash key, or a location on your network. Then follow the same steps: click **File**, click **Import and Export**, and click the **Import Favorites** option on the **Import/Export Selection** page.

If you want even more control over your Favorites, I recommend a wonderful utility called Powermarks (*http://www.kaylon.com*), which I use to manage my list of favorite Web sites. It allows you to search through your collection of Favorites (something you can't do with Internet Explorer). It also allows you to export your Favorites collection to a file or save it on a special Web server, making it easy to move to your new computer.

- **Internet Explorer cookies.** Cookies can be a big help in everyday browsing. The Files and Settings Transfer Wizard transfers all cookies for you. You can back up your cookie collection if you prefer by using the Import and Export utility in Internet Explorer. Follow the same instructions as you used to save your Favorites, choosing the **Export Cookies** option on the **Import/Export Selection** page.

- **Saved passwords.** If you're like most people, you probably have dozens of passwords that you use on the Web, for everything from online banking to shopping for books to posting on a bulletin board about your favorite hobbies. The Files and Settings Transfer Wizard does not transfer any passwords or form data you've saved in Internet Explorer. You'll need to enter this information manually on your new PC.

  To help keep track of passwords and logon information, I highly recommend RoboForm (*http://www.roboform.com*). It allows you to create truly random passwords that are unique for each Web site you visit, keeps track of the list of passwords so that you can log on automatically when you return, and helps fill in forms on Web pages. The program has Backup and Restore options to help you avoid losing this crucial information.

- **The Windows Address Book.** Outlook Express keeps all of your saved e-mail addresses in a file you open with the Windows Address Book program. The Files and Settings Transfer Wizard copies this file to your new computer automatically. If you prefer to move these saved addresses manually, open Outlook Express and click the Address Book button. (If the toolbar isn't visible, click **Tools**, and then click **Address Book**.) From the Windows Address Book, click **File**, click **Export**, and then click **Address Book (WAB)....** Save the file in a safe place. To restore the saved addresses, open Windows Address Book again, click **File**, and then click **Import**.

● **Outlook Express messages and settings.** The Files and Settings Transfer Wizard copies all of your saved Outlook Express e-mail messages to your new PC, along with saved settings and details for each e-mail account (minus the password). However, Outlook Express doesn't include any way for you to back up your messages or export them directly to a new PC.

I'm a strong believer in making regular backup copies of important information. If you use Outlook Express, you can back up your messages, settings, and address book using a free program called OEBackup (*http://www.oehelp.com/OEBackup)*. This program is also ideal if you want to move all of your e-mail to your new PC. Copy the backup file to a USB flash key or to a location on your network. Install a fresh copy of OEBackup on your new PC, and use the program's Restore feature to put everything in its proper place.

NOTE When you open Outlook Express and click File, you'll see an Export choice on the menu. This option is only useful when you install Microsoft Outlook (part of Microsoft Office) and you want to move messages from Outlook Express to your new Outlook data file. This Export utility doesn't work with any other e-mail programs, nor can you use it to transfer e-mail messages to another copy of Outlook Express on another computer.

● **Microsoft Office program settings.** The Files and Settings Transfer Wizard migrates settings from versions of Office up to and including Office XP. However, you'll encounter errors and you may find that your Outlook data is unavailable if you use the wizard on a computer with Office 2003. In fact, with Office 2000, Office XP, or Office 2003, you'll have much better luck using the Microsoft Office Save My Settings Wizard, which was expressly designed for use with Office. Just as with the Files and Settings Transfer Wizard, you run this wizard on your old computer first and save the results as a file. You then run the wizard on your new computer and open the saved file to complete the transfer. You'll find the shortcut to the Save My Settings Wizard in the Microsoft Office Tools group on the All Programs menu (or the Programs menu, if your old computer is running an earlier version of Windows).

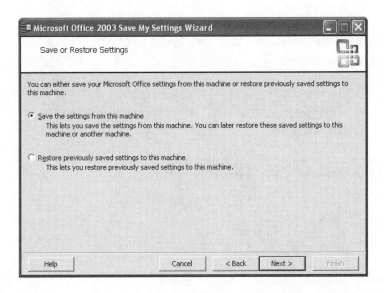

Choose your transfer method

You're now ready to run the Files and Settings Transfer Wizard. The exact procedure depends on how you choose to make the transfer.

You'll need to run the wizard twice, once on the old computer and once on the new computer. If your old computer is running a version of Windows other than Windows XP, use the Windows XP CD to get the wizard started. (If the CD isn't available, you can create a disk that runs the wizard.) Insert the CD in the old computer's CD-ROM drive, and wait for the **Welcome to Microsoft Windows XP** screen. (If this screen doesn't appear, open My Computer and double-click the CD drive icon.)

TIP   What do you do if you're planning to use your old monitor with your new PC? I suggest that you set up a network connection between the two computers and choose the option to save your files and settings to a folder or drive. Get the new PC running first. Leave it powered on as you disconnect the monitor and connect it to your old PC. Run the Files and Settings Transfer Wizard on your old PC, and save the resulting file in the Shared Documents folder on the new PC. You can now reconnect the monitor to the new PC, start the wizard, and open the saved settings from your Shared Documents folder.

Click **Perform additional tasks,** and then click **Transfer files and settings**.

On the new computer (and on the old one, if it's running Windows XP), click **Start**, click **All Programs**, click **Accessories**, and then click **System Tools**. Finally, click **Files and Settings Transfer Wizard**.

After the wizard starts, click **Next** to skip past the its opening page. When you see the **Which Computer Is This?** page, shown here, you're ready to begin in earnest. Choose one of the methods below and get started.

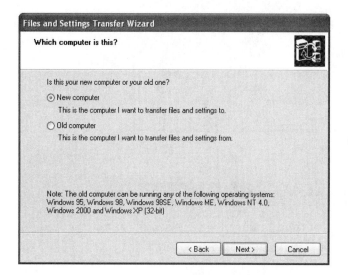

- **Transfer directly over a network** If you followed the instructions in the previous chapter to set up a network connection between the old computer and the new one, you can transfer all your files and settings directly. After you reinstall all your old programs on the new computer, you should be ready to go.

CAUTION If you plan to use a network, you *must* follow the instructions exactly as I outline them here. In particular, you must run the wizard on the new computer first. If you skip this step and start with the old computer, the wizard will give you an error message, or the Home or small office network choice won't be available for you to select.

Start by running the wizard on the new PC. When you reach the **Which Computer Is This?** page, choose **New Computer** and then click **Next**. The Windows Firewall will intercept your request and display the Windows Security Alert dialog box shown here. Click **Unblock** to continue.

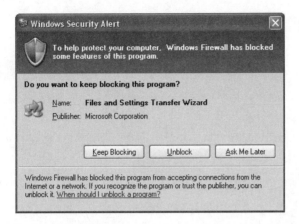

On the **Do you have a Windows XP CD?** page, choose **I will use the wizard from the Windows XP CD** and click **Next**. (If you don't have the CD at hand, choose the option to make a Wizard Disk. You'll need a blank, formatted disk or a USB flash memory key for this task.)

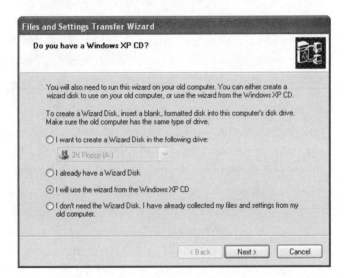

For now, you're through with the new computer. Leave this dialog box open, and go to the old computer. To continue, skip ahead to the next section, "Customize your transfer options."

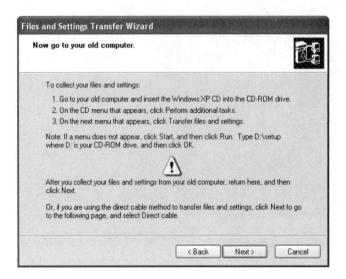

- **Transfer directly using a direct cable connection.** This option refers to a "null modem" cable (sometimes called a LapLink cable) that connects the two computers' serial ports. Most people don't have one of these cables, and they're painfully slow anyway. I don't recommend this option. If you decide to use this connection method anyway, connect the computers first, using the serial cable, and then follow the instructions above as if you were using a network.

- **Save files and settings on removable media** If you don't have a network, you can use the Files and Settings Transfer Wizard with removable media. This method works as long as you have some way to save the files and settings from the old computer so that you can physically carry them to the new one. Given the size of the files involved, I recommend media with a capacity of at least 100 MB per disk, such as Zip disks or a USB flash drive. (Don't even think about trying to use floppy disks. They don't have enough storage capacity to handle the job, and you're likely to need dozens of diskettes to finish the job.)

  If you plan to use this method, start with the old computer. Skip ahead to the next section, "Customize your transfer options."

- **Save files and settings on a local or network hard disk** This method is simple and straightforward. It works best if you have an external hard drive; in that case, you run the wizard on the old computer and save your files and settings to a folder on the hard drive. After the wizard finishes its work, you connect the hard drive to the new computer, start the wizard, and point to the files you saved. The procedure works in roughly the same fashion if you have access to a location on your network where you can share files. In that case, however, you're better off using your network connection directly rather than saving your settings and files

  If you plan to use this method, start with the old computer. Skip ahead to the next section, "Customize your transfer options."

❑ Customize your transfer options

When you run the wizard on your old computer, you have the option to specify which files and settings you want to transfer. Your goal is to make the process as efficient and effective as possible. Follow these steps:

1 Go to the old computer, and start the Files and Settings Transfer Wizard. Click **Next** to skip the wizard's opening page. On the **Which computer is this?** page, click **Old computer** and then click **Next**.

2 On the **Select a transfer method** page, shown on the next page, choose the option that corresponds to the transfer method you have chosen:

- **Direct cable.** This option is grayed out and unavailable unless you have already connected your computers and run the wizard on the new computer.

- **Home or small office network.** If this option is unavailable, or if you receive an error message when you choose it, go back to the new computer and verify that the wizard is running already, as described in the previous section. If you still can't connect, you'll need to troubleshoot your network connection.

- **Floppy drive or other removable media.** The drop-down list below this option shows all available removable devices installed in your computer, including floppy drives, Zip drives, and USB flash keys. If you choose this option, make sure the same type of drive is available on the new computer.

● **Other.** Select this option if you want to save the files to a location on your computer, on your network, or to a removable hard drive, such as a USB drive. Click **Browse** to choose the location where you want to save the files.

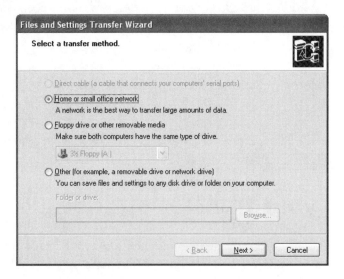

3   On the **What do you want to transfer?** screen, shown at the top of the next page, select the combination of settings and files you want to transfer.

● **Settings only.** This option transfers your Windows settings (desktop, colors, fonts, and so on) and settings for various programs. For all transfer methods except a floppy drive, this option also includes all your e-mail accounts and messages from Outlook Express, along with the Windows Address Book.

● **Files only.** This option transfers all files from specific folders, including My Documents and the Desktop. It also searches all other folders on your entire computer for files that have extensions from the list shown in the box on the right.

● **Both files and settings.** This is the default selection. It includes both categories.

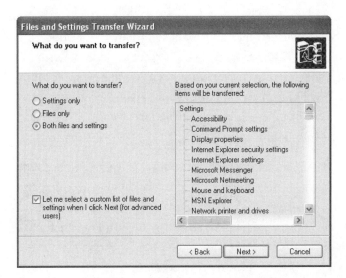

If you want to pick and choose from items on the list of available settings and files, click the check box to the left of **Let me select a custom list of files and settings**. Don't be intimidated by the warning that this is for advanced users; anyone can use this option, and it isn't particularly difficult to figure it out.

4 Click **Next** to continue. If you clicked the option to customize the list of files and settings, you'll see a dialog box like the one shown in Figure 1. Add or remove any items if you want, and then click **Next**.

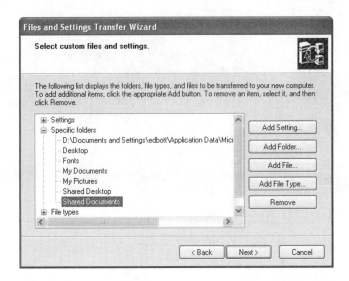

Figure 1 *Use this dialog box to fine-tune the list of files and settings that the wizard transfers for you.*

For most people, the wizard works best if you choose the default settings. In one specific set of circumstances, however, you might want to modify these options. If your old computer was running Windows XP and you had set up multiple user accounts, you need to run the wizard once from your main Administrator account, using the default settings. This picks up the files from your personal profile (those in your My Documents folder, for instance). It also grabs files in shared locations and searches the hard drive for other data files.

To get the files for a second user account, you need to set up a matching account on the new computer, log on to each computer using this additional account, and run the wizard again. When you do this, you don't want the wizard to retrieve shared files or search the hard drive again. Instead, choose the option to customize your settings. On the **Select custom files and settings** page, click the first entry under the **File types** heading and click **Remove**. Repeat this process for all the entries in the **File types** list. Then click **Shared Desktop** under the **Specific folders** heading and click **Remove**. Do the same for **Shared Documents**. This customized list will pick up only settings and files that belong to the logged-on user account.

CAUTION When you use this option, make sure you log on to the correct user account on the new computer!

5   Click **Next** to continue. You may see warnings related to settings for specific programs.

6   If you chose a removable media device as your transfer method, the wizard calculates how much storage space will be required for the options you selected and displays the results for you. If you have sufficient space on your removable media, click **OK** to continue; otherwise, click **Cancel** and restart the wizard, choosing a different transfer method.

7 If you are using a network to complete the transfer, a pair of matching dialog boxes pop up. The wizard displays a randomly selected password on the new computer (like the one shown first here). To continue, enter that password in the Password dialog box on the old computer, also shown here. This is a security precaution that prevents someone from using this wizard to try to steal files from your old computer without your permission.

8 After you finish these steps, the wizard begins collecting your files and settings. On a computer that includes lots of files to transfer, this process can take hours, so be patient. Follow the prompts to complete the wizard.

You're almost done.

☐ Make the move

If you chose the option to transfer files and setting over your network, the Files and Settings Transfer Wizard handles everything for you automatically. On both the old computer and the new computer, you see dialog boxes that offer a rough indication of the status of the process.

If you saved your files and settings to removable media or to a hard disk, follow these steps:

1 Go to the new computer, start the Files and Settings Transfer Wizard (if it's not already running), and follow the prompts, specifying that this is the new computer.

2 On the **Do you have a Windows XP CD?** page, click the check box to the left of **I don't need the Wizard Disk. I have already collected my files and settings from my old computer**. Click **Next**.

3 On the **Where are the files and settings?** page, click to select the location where your files are stored and click **Next** to continue.

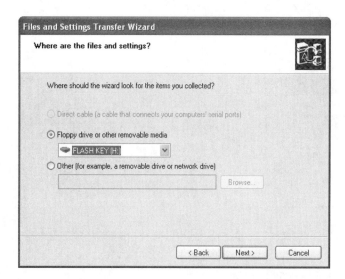

The wizard handles the rest of the details automatically. If necessary, you'll be prompted to supply additional media.

After the transfer is complete, click **Finish**, log off, and log back on. All the files and settings from your old computer should be ready for you to work with on your new computer.

If you have two or more user accounts on your old computer, log on to the second account and run through the wizard again. Pay special attention to the instructions in the "Customize your transfer options" section, earlier in this chapter.

Test and troubleshoot

The Files and Settings Transfer Wizard is thorough, but it isn't perfect. Now that you've finished transferring everything to your new PC, make a special effort to verify that everything is working properly. In particular, check your e-mail accounts (you'll need to supply a password for each one), your saved messages, and your Address Book. After you finish setting up your hardware and installing all your favorite programs on the new computer—which we'll do in the next two chapters— you can make sure that the data files associated with those programs are working properly.

Don't be in too much of a hurry to delete the files from your old computer. It's possible that the wizard missed a few files. After you get to the end of this book, give your new computer a thorough workout for a week or so, until you're certain that you've got all the files you need. At that point, you can safely delete your files from the old computer.

Step 5: **Set Up Printers, Digital Cameras, and Other Hardware**

In this chapter, I show you how to set up the hardware that allows your computer to do truly interesting things, like capture pictures from your digital camera, print those images on photo-quality paper, mix and burn your own CDs, and synchronize your address book with a handheld PDA (or personal digital assistant).

Your new PC may already include some internal hardware upgrades, such as a DVD burner or a surround sound audio system. Other hardware add-ons are external, designed to be plugged into a USB or 1394 (FireWire) port. Before any piece of hardware—internal or external—can work with your new PC, it needs a *device driver*. A device driver is a small piece of software that tells Windows how to work with that device. If you plug in a new device without installing the correct driver, Windows can tell that an unknown device is available, but it can't do anything with it.

The biggest challenge in setting up hardware is to find the right drivers for all your hardware devices and install them correctly. In this chapter, I'll show you how to set up your printer and configure it for sharing over a network. You'll also fine-tune your display, get your CD and DVD drives working properly, tune up your speakers and sound card, and get external devices like cameras and scanners working properly.

☑ Checklist:

❑ **Take inventory (page 130).** Use Device Manager to identify any problem devices and to get details about installed drivers.

❑ **Create a System Restore point (page 133).** This is a crucial step before making major changes to your PC. If a new driver causes problems, remove it and "roll back" to the old one.

❑ **Prepare to install and update devices (page 134).** Gather drivers and learn the do's and don'ts of proper installation.

❑ **Update hardware drivers, if necessary (page 141).** Windows Update offers quick access to signed, compatible drivers. You can also download and install updates manually.

❑ **Fine-tune your display (page 143).** Make sure your video adapter and monitor are working properly.

❑ **Check CD and DVD drives (page 144).** Pay special attention to recordable drives and the software for playing back DVDs.

❑ **Tune up your sound settings (page 145).** The default settings assume you have two small speakers on your desktop. Tweaking some advanced settings can result in better sound.

❑ **Set up and share a printer (page 147).** Connect a printer, get it working, and allow other people on your network to use it.

❑ **Test and troubleshoot (page 150).** After installing each device, make sure it's working properly. If you encounter problems, fix them now before moving on.

☐ Take inventory

How many devices are installed on your computer right now? The list of installed devices might surprise you. Your new PC's innards are complex, and even a stripped-down system might consist of 60 or more devices; most of these are internal components that the operating system works with constantly but you never see.

To see a full list of devices installed on your computer, use the Windows Device Manager.

1   Click **Start** and then click **Control Panel**.

2   Click **Performance and Maintenance** and then click **See basic information about your computer**. (If you see only a collection of icons in Control Panel, click **Switch to Category View** in the list of tasks under the **Control Panel** heading at the left.) The System Properties dialog box opens.

3   Click the Hardware tab and then click **Device Manager**.

This utility, shown in Figure 1, provides a full inventory of all installed devices—internal and external—organized by category. It also provides access to tools that allow you to view details about installed drivers, troubleshoot problem devices, and update installed drivers.

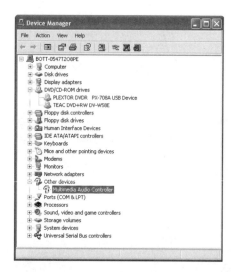

Figure 1   *Click the plus sign to the left of any device category to see devices within that category. Problem devices are identified with a yellow question mark or a red X.*

Don't get bogged down looking through Device Manager right now. Your goal is to identify any devices that are not working properly. In Device Manager, look at the small icon to the left of the device name. A red X over the icon means the device has been disabled. A yellow question mark indicates an unknown device. A yellow exclamation point means the device has another sort of problem, such as a conflict with another installed device.

If you see any problem devices, double-click the device name (or right-click the device name and click **Properties**) and read the details in the **Device status** section on the General tab. If you see a **Reinstall Driver...** or **Troubleshoot** button, Windows may be able to steer you toward a solution; click the button to see more recommendations or to attempt repairs. (See the final section of this chapter, "Test and troubleshoot," for additional advice on how to solve hardware-related problems.)

CAUTION If you're having a problem with a device, you might be tempted to start tinkering with options on the properties dialog box for that device. Don't! Choosing an incorrect configuration might get the problem device working again by disabling another device. Murphy's Law says anything that can go wrong, will. That's especially true when you mess with settings you don't fully understand. If you tinker too much, you run the risk of preventing your PC from starting properly. Be extra careful when troubleshooting hardware.

You can also use Device Manager to find details about the driver Windows itself is using for a device. This information is particularly useful when you find a driver available for download at a hardware maker's Web site and you want to know whether the currently installed driver is newer than the one you're thinking of downloading. Double-click the device name in the list of installed devices and click the **Driver** tab on the properties dialog box. The information at the top of this dialog box tells you which company provided the driver, when it was released, its version number, and whether the driver is digitally signed.

A device driver may actually consist of multiple files. For technical details about each of the files in a driver package, click the **Driver Details...** button. For most normal hardware setup tasks, you won't need this information; it's most useful when you're working with support personnel from the device manufacturer to resolve a technical problem.

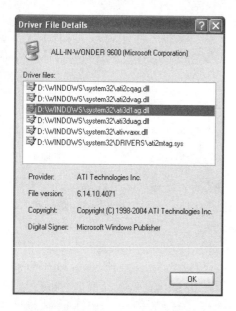

If you have any devices that aren't working, try to fix the problem now, before you move on to the remainder of this chapter. If the built-in Windows troubleshooters can't resolve the problem for you, contact the PC manufacturer to see if they can help you resolve the issues. Once everything is working right, you can continue.

Create a System Restore point

The System Restore feature creates a "snapshot" of your current system configuration. When you install a signed device driver, Windows automatically creates a restore point for you. If you install a driver that causes problems, you can run System Restore and return to the previous configuration, minus the problematic driver.

Even though Windows will create restore points for you at several points in the process you're about to go through, I recommend that you create a manual restore point now, while your system is still clean and uncluttered with any new drivers. With this precaution in place, you'll know you have a working configuration to go back to in the event of problems. Follow these steps:

1 Click **Start**, and then click **Help and Support**.

2 In the Help and Support Center, under the **Pick a task** heading, click **Undo changes to your computer with System Restore**.

3 On the **Welcome to System Restore** page, click **Create a restore point** and click **Next**.

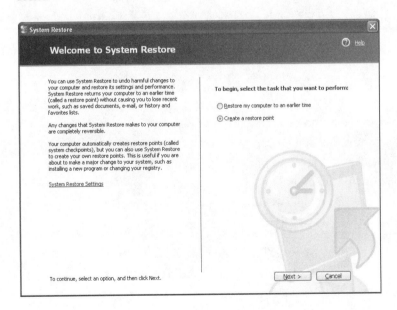

4   On the **Create a Restore Point** page, click in the **Restore point description** box
and enter a short label to identify why you're creating this restore point. Click
Create.

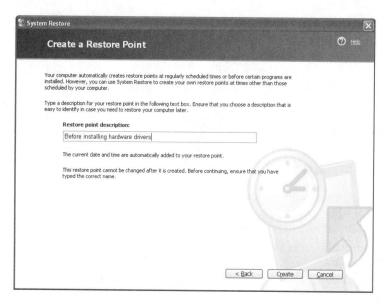

5   The **Restore Point Created** page confirms that you've successfully created the
restore point. Click **Close**.

☐ Prepare to install and update devices

If you followed my advice at the beginning of this book, you've already gathered
the documentation and software CDs you need to install any hardware you already
own. (If you skipped over this step, go back to "Round up your hardware manuals
and drivers," which begins on page 6.) If you purchased any new external devices
with your new PC, have those manuals close at hand also. For each device you plan
to install, ask yourself three questions:

● **Is it compatible with Windows XP?** Some hardware devices simply don't
work with Windows XP. This is especially true of older products. If you own a
device that was designed in 2001 or earlier (even if you purchased it later), be
suspicious. Some manufacturers made a conscious choice not to develop
Windows XP–compatible drivers for older devices. If you can identify any such

devices now, you can save yourself hours of frustration and avoid potential problems.

- **Is a digitally signed driver available?** Hardware drivers that have passed Microsoft's rigorous hardware tests are digitally signed by Microsoft. This provides a strong assurance that the drivers will not cause your system to crash. Unsigned drivers have not passed these tests and might cause stability problems, up to and including unpredictable crashes.

- **Do you have the most up-to-date driver files?** Hardware manufacturers routinely update drivers and supporting software, especially for printers and scanners. The installation CD included with a device on store shelves today may contain software that is already a year or two old. When in doubt, look for a date, a revision number, or other version information on the CD and compare those details to the latest downloads available at the manufacturer's Web site.

The best way to check whether a specific device is compatible with Windows XP is to look in the Windows Catalog, a continually updated, Web-based list of hardware and software that has been tested with Windows XP. To reach the Windows Catalog, go to *http://www.microsoft.com/windows/catalog*; or click **Start**, then click **Help and Support**, and finally click **Find compatible hardware and software for Windows XP** in the Help and Support Center.

On the Windows Catalog home page, you can click the Hardware tab and then browse by category if you're shopping for a new device. To look up the name of a device you already own, enter all or part of the product name or the manufacturer's name in the **Search** box and then click **Go**. If you see the Designed for Windows XP logo or the text label "Compatible with Windows XP" next to a product name, you know the product has been tested by Microsoft and certified to work properly with Windows XP. Some items in the list include clickable links that take you to the manufacturer's Web site, where you'll find more details. In some cases, the details page for a product also includes links to the latest downloadable drivers.

If you can't find a product listed in the Windows Catalog, that doesn't mean it's incompatible with Windows XP. Before you try to install the device, however, you should verify independently that a compatible driver is available. Look in the printed documentation for the product or on the manufacturer's Web site for this information.

Most of the devices you'll use to expand the capabilities of your new PC are designed to be plugged in (typically to a USB port) when they're needed and removed when they're no longer required. The first time you use a device, you install the necessary drivers. After that, Windows automatically loads the correct drivers and configures the device when you connect it, without requiring that you restart your computer. The following list identifies some factors you need to take into consideration with specific types of external devices. (Later in this chapter, I'll show you how to test and, if necessary, configure internal devices that came with your computer.)

- **Keyboards and mice** Windows includes drivers that work with most types of input devices, including mice with wheels. The basic drivers enable some custom buttons found on custom keyboards, including those that control speaker volume and launch your browser. If your keyboard or mouse includes more exotic features, you'll need to install custom drivers and configuration software to enable the extra bells and whistles.

- **Digital cameras** Windows XP includes a slick, easy-to-use wizard that works with most modern digital cameras. Some cameras—notably those made by Kodak—include custom drivers and software that offer a greater range of configuration options. If your camera includes its own software and drivers, set a System Restore point before running Setup. Try the custom software out; if you don't like it, uninstall the software and use System Restore to switch back to your previous configuration. You can then choose the standard Windows XP digital imaging tools.

TIP   If you have an older camera that doesn't connect directly with Windows XP, don't give up right away. Get an external reader that uses the same memory card format as the camera. Instead of hooking the camera directly to your new PC, you can remove the memory card and insert it into the reader. In this configuration, Windows XP uses the Scanner and Camera Wizard just as if you had connected the camera directly.

- **Scanners** Scanners present some of the same issues as digital cameras. Before you install custom software provided by the hardware manufacturer, see if the Scanner and Camera Wizard will do the job just as well. If your scanner has advanced features such as an automated sheet feeder, the extra software may be required.

- **Portable music players** Most devices in this category include a program designed to help you synchronize the player's collection with the digital music on your PC. With devices that support the Windows Media Audio (WMA) standard, you may be able to use Windows Media Player instead. Apple's iPod is a noteworthy exception; you need to install Apple's iTunes software to perform synchronization. Check out your player's requirements carefully before installing any software or drivers, and make sure you update to the most recent version.

  > **TIP**   Windows XP Service Pack 2 includes Windows Media Player 9 Series. An updated version, Windows Media Player 10, offers much easier support for some portable devices. Check the details at *http://www.microsoft.com/windowsmedia*

- **Removable disk drives** If you have a standard storage device such as an external hard drive that supports the USB 2.0 standard, it should not require any special software or drivers. You should be able to plug the device in directly and see it as an icon in My Computer. Some specialized storage devices such as Zip drives may require extra software to enable features such as the capability to format a disk.

- **Personal digital assistants (PDAs)** These handheld devices are designed to keep personal information (address books, calendars, e-mail, and so on) synchronized with information stored on your PC. For a PDA that uses the Palm operating system, or OS (*http://www.palmsource.com*), you'll need to install the Palm Desktop software. Pocket PCs (*http://www.microsoft.com/windowsmobile*) use Windows Mobile software and require that you install Microsoft ActiveSync software to enable synchronization. In either case, look for the CD that came with the device and then check for more recent updates.

After you've gathered driver disks and downloaded any required updates, you're ready to begin. Later in this chapter, I offer detailed advice for specific types of hardware. For each new device, follow these steps:

1 If the device includes a Setup program (either on CD or as a downloaded file), run this program to install the driver files and any supporting software *before* plugging in the device.

> **TIP** When in doubt, read the installation instructions. With some devices, you may be instructed to plug in the device first and supply the driver CD later.

2 Plug the device into an available port. Because this is the first time you've plugged in the device, Windows XP tries to identify the device and locate a compatible driver for it. You see a series of status messages in the notification area, located to the right of the taskbar, as the Windows Plug and Play process goes through its library of installed drivers.

If Windows finds a compatible driver already available (such as the one you just added), it installs the driver, configures the device for you, and completes the installation. If Windows cannot locate compatible drivers, it starts the Found New Hardware Wizard.

3 The wizard asks you if you want to search for an updated driver on Windows Update. Choose one of the **Yes** options and click **Next**.

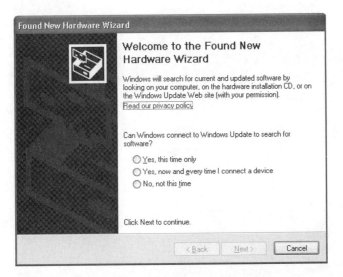

4 If Windows Update finds a compatible driver, it installs the software and configures the device for you. If not, the wizard presents the two options shown here:

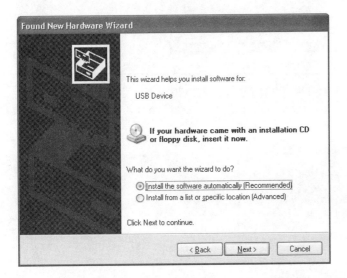

- **Install the software automatically (Recommended)** Use this option if you ran a Setup program to install the driver first, or if the driver is on a CD-ROM or floppy disk. Insert the correct CD or floppy disk, if needed, and click **Next**.

● **Install from a list or specific location (Advanced)** Choose this option if you downloaded the driver files and didn't run a Setup program first. Click **Next** to continue. On the page that follows, click the check box to the left of Include this location in the search. Click **Browse** and select the location where you saved the downloaded driver files. Click **Next** to continue.

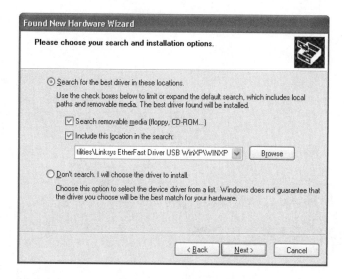

5   If the driver file you're trying to install is digitally signed, it should install automatically. If not, you'll see a stern warning message like the one shown here.

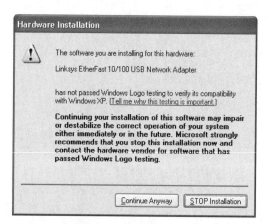

If you're certain the driver is compatible with Windows XP and that a signed driver is not available, click **Continue Anyway**. Windows automatically creates a restore point for you, so that you can undo the change if the driver causes problems later.

6 When you reach the final step of the Found New Hardware Wizard, read the status message carefully. If the driver installation was successful, click **Finish** to close the wizard and begin using the new device. If the wizard reports any problems, troubleshoot them now, or roll back to the previous configuration using the System Restore feature.

Repeat the above steps for any additional devices you plan to install.

CAUTION Pay close attention to any warning about unsigned drivers. Digitally signed drivers really are safer, because they've been tested for compatibility with Windows XP. I can testify from firsthand experience that unsigned drivers can cause your system to become unstable or even crash. If you choose to install an unsigned driver, try to use the device in question extensively over the next few days and be alert for problems. If necessary, run the System Restore utility and roll back your system configuration to the old driver (which was saved for you automatically).

☐ Update hardware drivers, if necessary

How do you know whether you have the best driver available for a hardware device? Start by checking Windows Update. When hardware manufacturers release new drivers that pass Microsoft's stringent testing, the digitally signed drivers show up when you visit Windows Update manually (they aren't delivered by way of the Automatic Updates feature). Click **Start**, then click **All Programs**, and click **Windows Update**. Click **Custom Install** to scan for available updates. The software compares the list of hardware devices installed on your computer with the list of available updates; if it finds a match, download and install the new driver by clicking **Select optional hardware updates** in the left pane of the Windows Update screen. Drivers you download from Windows Update install automatically.

Not all driver updates make it to Windows Update. If you suspect that an updated driver is available for a device currently installed on your computer, visit the device manufacturer's Web site and search in the Downloads or Support section. You may need to use Device Manager (described earlier in this chapter) to determine the version number of the currently installed driver and compare it with the driver available for download.

After you download an updated driver, you need to install it manually. To help you accomplish this task, use the Hardware Update Wizard, which is remarkably similar to the Found New Hardware Wizard.

CAUTION Don't obsess over having the absolute latest driver at all times. If your device is working, and you notice that a new driver is available, read the manufacturer's description of what the new driver does and decide for yourself whether you really need the update.

Earlier in this book, I recommended that you create a Downloads folder as a convenient storage location for programs you acquire from the Web. If you followed this advice, why not also create a Drivers subfolder here? When you download a new driver from a hardware maker's Web site, save the file into its own subfolder in this location. If you ever need to reinstall the driver, you'll have no problem finding it.

1   Click **Start**, right-click **My Computer**, and click **Properties**. In the System Properties dialog box, click the Hardware tab and then click **Device Manager**.

2   In Device Manager, click the plus sign to the left of the category that contains the device whose driver you want to update. Double-click the entry for the device and click **Update Driver** on the **Driver** tab.

3   In the Hardware Update Wizard, click **Install from a list or specific location (Advanced)**. Click **Next** to continue.

4   Click **Don't search. I will choose the driver to install.** Click **Next** to continue.

5   The **Select the device driver you want to install for this hardware** dialog box shows the currently installed driver. Click **Have Disk...** and click **Browse...** to specify the location of the new drivers you downloaded. Click **OK**.

6   The contents of the dialog box show a list of drivers that are compatible with the installed device. Look for a green check mark to the left of the driver name and a message at the bottom of the dialog box that indicates the driver is digitally signed.

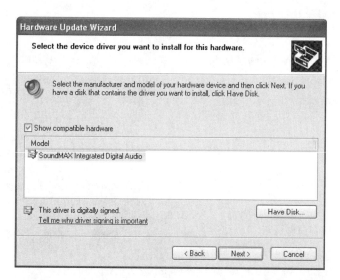

7   Click **Next** to install the driver, and then click **Finish** to complete the wizard.

☐ Fine-tune your display

Your video subsystem—the combination of a display adapter and a monitor—probably has more impact on your personal productivity than any other device. If you use a conventional CRT monitor (the not-so-thin type with a picture tube), pay special attention to the refresh rate, which defines how many times per minute the video adapter redraws the display. If this value is too low, the result is an unpleasant flickering, which can cause long-term eyestrain and fatigue. In addition, poorly written video display drivers are among the most common causes of Windows crashes and instability. To deal with both of these problems, make sure your new PC is using a signed video driver and that your monitor is set to the proper refresh rate.

To view and adjust the settings for your video adapter, follow these steps:

1 Right-click any empty space on the desktop and click **Properties**. (Alternatively, you can open Control Panel, click **Appearance and Themes**, and click **Display**.)

2 On the Settings tab, click **Advanced**.

3 Click the Adapter tab. The details in the **Adapter Information** section provide technical information that isn't particularly useful.

> **NOTE** This section focuses strictly on the hardware settings of your video subsystem. In "Step 7: Personalize and Organize," which begins on page 172, I explain how to adjust screen resolution, color depth, and other more cosmetic settings.

Two other sections of this dialog box, however, are potentially useful:

■ Click **Properties** to display information about the installed video driver. On the **Driver** tab, click **Update** to check for a newer driver.

■ Click **List All Modes...** to display a list of supported resolutions and refresh rates. Make a note of the refresh rates supported at the resolution and color depth you plan to use. Click **OK** to close the List All Modes dialog box.

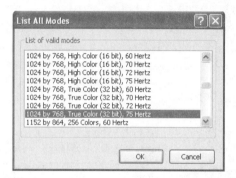

4   Click the **Monitor** tab to display the dialog box shown below. In the **Screen refresh rate** list, check the current refresh rate setting. If you have a flat-panel (LCD) monitor, this value should be set to 60 Hertz. For a conventional CRT monitor, set the refresh rate to the highest value for your chosen screen resolution, using the information you jotted down in the previous step.

5   Click **OK** to close the monitor properties dialog box, and then click **OK** to close the **Display Properties** dialog box.

Don't worry about updating your monitor driver. Unless you have unusual hardware with special capabilities, a monitor "driver" is typically just a file that contains a few settings to allow a wider range of refresh rates and resolutions. If the Display Settings dialog box shows Plug and Play Monitor as the device type, you can move on.

⬜ Check CD and DVD drives

It's easy enough to check the basic operation of a CD or DVD drive. Insert any data CD into the drive and open it in My Computer. If Windows Explorer shows the disc's contents, the drive is working. Two additional features are worth checking at this point:

- **Do you have a recordable CD or DVD drive?** Right-click the drive icon in My Computer and look for a **Recording** tab on the properties dialog box. If you plan to use the built-in Windows XP CD-burning capabilities, select the check box to the left of **Enable CD recording on this drive**. Clear the check box if you have a third-party program you plan to use instead. Note the write speed selection in the list at the bottom of this dialog box. If you encounter problems burning CDs, try moving this setting to a lower value.

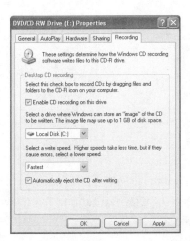

NOTE Windows XP does not include DVD-burning capabilities. If you have a DVD burner, you can use the built-in Windows XP tools to create custom CDs, but you'll need third-party software to burn DVDs.

- **Do you plan to play back DVDs?** Windows XP does not include DVD-playback capabilities. Most DVD drives include a software add-on that enables DVD capabilities. If your DVD drive was installed at the factory, pop in a DVD and see if it plays in Windows Media Player. If the Play DVD menu is missing, you'll need to find the required software and install it.

Tune up your sound settings

I assume you've already installed the correct drivers for your sound card and you've hooked up your speakers correctly. If so, you've already heard an assortment of PC-related sounds. To finish setting up the hardware, open Control Panel, click **Sounds, Speech, and Audio Devices,** and click **Adjust the system volume**. This choice opens the Sounds and Audio Devices Properties dialog box and displays the Volume tab. I recommend that you click the check box to the left of **Place volume icon in the** taskbar. This option gives you ready access to a volume icon so you can mute the sound completely or adjust the volume when playing music or listening to audio on a Web page.

Click **Advanced...** if you have a speaker arrangement other than the default option of two stereo speakers on the desktop. If you have speakers integrated into your monitor or keyboard, for instance, you'll find those options here.

If you hear no sounds, try these troubleshooting pointers:

● Check the connection from the computer to your speakers. Is the cable plugged into the correct output jack on the sound card?

● Are your speakers powered on? Most computer speakers require AC power, and some have a power switch. Make sure they're plugged in and turned on.

● Open the mixer to see if any inputs are muted. In the **Sounds and Audio Devices Properties** dialog box, click **Advanced** to open the **Play Control** dialog box shown here. Your computer has multiple inputs for different types of audio. If the **Mute** button beneath any of these inputs is selected, clear its check box, and then use the volume sliders to adjust each input separately.

> **NOTE** The software for some high-end sound cards replaces the standard Play Control dialog box shown here with a custom audio mixer. Although it may look different, the basic function should be exactly the same.

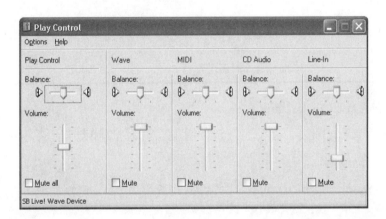

Set up and share a printer

Just about everyone has a printer. If you're passionate about printouts, in fact, you probably have a couple of printers—one for simple documents and another for printing photos on glossy paper. If your printer is less than two years old, Windows XP probably includes the hardware drivers you need to get up and running. If the printer uses a USB connection and you're certain it's fully compatible with Windows XP, you can plug it in now with reasonable confidence that Windows Plug and Play will install the correct driver and get it working quickly.

If your printer is more than two years old—or if it's a multifunction machine that scans and faxes in addition to putting ink on paper—you'll probably need to install some supporting files first. Look for the CD that came with the printer. After verifying that the software on the CD is intended for Windows XP, go ahead and run the Setup program from the CD.

TIP   Updating the software for a multi-function device can pose a challenge if you're limited to dial-up Internet access. I've seen drivers that weigh in at 75 MB or more, which could take hours to download over a slow connection. If you're not willing to wait that long, install the driver from the original CD that came with your device. Then contact the manufacturer and ask them to send you an updated CD containing the most recent drivers.

If you have an older printer that uses a parallel connection instead of a USB port, follow these steps to install the printer. Make sure the printer is powered off when you start.

1 Connect one end of a parallel cable to your printer and plug the connector at the other end of the cable into your PC's parallel port.

2 Turn the printer's power on.

3 Click **Start,** and then click **Printers and Faxes**.

4 In the Printers and Faxes folder, under the **Printer Tasks** heading on the left, click **Add a printer**.

5 Follow the wizard's prompts. When you reach the dialog box shown below, select the **Automatically detect and install my Plug and Play printer** check box.

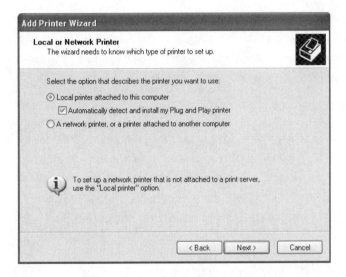

If you prefer to install the printer driver manually, clear the Plug and Play check box and click **Next**. On the **Install Printer Software** page, select a manufacturer and model name from the respective lists, as shown here. If you have a CD that has a signed, recent driver, click **Have Disk...** and browse to the correct location. Click **Windows Update** if you want to first check for an updated printer driver from Microsoft's collection.

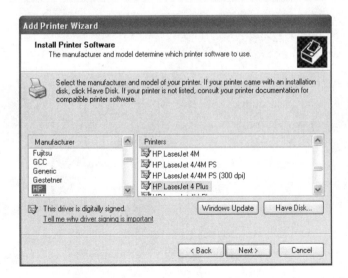

6 To allow other network users to share the local printer, click **Share name** when you reach the **Printer Sharing** page, and enter the name you want other people to see when they connect to the printer from another computer. Ideally, this name should consist of no more than 8 characters, without any spaces.

7 Follow the prompts to finish the wizard and install your printer.

If you created a shared printer, any network user can connect to it. In the **Printers and Faxes** dialog box, click **Add a Printer** again. This time, however, instead of clicking the **Local printer** option, click **A network printer, or a printer attached to another computer**. When you click **Next**, the wizard will search the network, find the shared printer, and download the correct driver from the computer to which the printer is connected.

When you add a new printer, local or network, the final step is to print a test page. I strongly recommend that you do this. If the page prints properly, you can move on to other tasks. If you hit any snags, a troubleshooter is one click away.

Test and troubleshoot

What happens when you plug in a new piece of hardware and it doesn't work properly? Before you do anything else, try unplugging and reconnecting the device. If you plugged it into a USB hub, try plugging it directly into a USB port on the computer. If that doesn't work, you have four options:

- **Use System Restore to undo the changes** If you just installed the device, you can immediately reverse all your changes. First, open Control Panel and click **Add or Remove Programs**. If the software package you installed is in this list, click to select it and then click **Remove**. Next, open the Help and Support Center and click **Undo changes to your computer with System Restore**. Choose the restore point created just before you installed the driver that's giving you problems.

- **Roll back to your old driver** If you updated to a new device driver and the update caused more problems than it fixed, you can ask Windows to remove the new driver and restore the old one. Open **Device Manager**, double-click the device name, select the **Driver** tab, and then click **Roll Back Driver**. You may need to restart your computer after doing this.

- **Disable the device** If the device isn't working right but isn't causing any other problems, consider disabling it temporarily. You can then talk with a technical support professional to come up with a more permanent solution. Open **Device Manager**, right-click the device name, and click **Disable**. After you fix the problem, you can repeat these steps, this time choosing **Enable** from the shortcut menu.

- **Uninstall the device** To remove all traces of a newly installed driver, open **Device Manager**, right-click the device name, and click **Uninstall** from the shortcut menu. Use this option if you didn't create a restore point (or if the only available restore point is too old to be useful to you) and you don't have a previous driver to roll back to. If you do this with a removable device, the device must be plugged in and turned on to be visible in Device Manager.

Step 6: Instant Productivity: Just Add Software

Your new PC includes an assortment of games, a CD player, and a Web browser. Those programs may keep you entertained, but they aren't exactly productivity tools. For that you'll need to reinstall the collection of programs from your old PC.

It's a tedious job, and there's no easy way to automate the process. In this chapter, I provide instructions on what to do before you install a program, where to look for updates, and how to set up programs properly. Once you get everything installed, you can create shortcuts for the programs you use most often and add them to places where you can get to them quickly: the Start menu, the Quick Launch toolbar, and the desktop.

Finally, I'll show you how to regain control when a newly installed program insists on trying to open files of a particular type. This is especially annoying when you add a program designed to help you manage digital music files. The last program you installed usually insists on taking charge of every file type it knows about. When you learn how file associations are stored, you can change them back.

☑ Checklist:

☐ **Remove unneeded software (page 154).** Your new PC may have arrived with an assortment of software. Weed out the programs you don't need.

☐ **Reinstall your favorite programs (page 156).** Start with your stack of program CDs and then move on to downloaded programs.

☐ **Update, update, update! (page 159)** Many programs include an option to check for updates, either manually or automatically. Take advantage of this option when you can.

☐ **Organize your program shortcuts (page 159).** Make your favorite programs easier to access by putting shortcuts on the Start menu, on the Quick Launch bar, and (if you must) on the desktop.

☐ **Review programs that start automatically (page 163).** Software that starts along with your computer can have negative effects on performance and stability. Trim the list of auto-starting programs.

☐ **Get file types and programs in sync (page 164).** When you double-click an MP3, does the wrong program open? Fix your file associations.

☐ **Set up your e-mail (page 167).** If the Files and Settings Wizard didn't import these settings for you, enter the information manually.

☐ **Test and troubleshoot (page 170).** After you confirm that everything's working right, you can move on to the final step.

Remove unneeded software

You haven't installed a single new program yet, so why should you be concerned about removing programs?

Most new PCs sold in the consumer market these days arrive with an assortment of preloaded programs. Often, these are introductory versions of programs designed to help you manage digital pictures or music files, burn CDs, or manage your personal finances. Your PC may include limited-time versions of antivirus software or subscriptions to a dial-up Internet service provider. The publishers of these programs cut deals with PC makers to put programs and offers on all new PCs, knowing that some people will try the software, like it, and pay for an upgrade to the full version.

I don't recommend that you arbitrarily remove everything that came with your new PC, but if you've given one of these programs a fair shake and decided you don't want or need it, or if you know that you prefer an alternative program, you should remove the unwanted software from your computer. Doing so frees up disk space, gets rid of background programs that may slow your new PC's performance, and prevents conflicts with other programs.

To remove programs, don't just delete the shortcuts on the Start menu and the desktop. Don't open Windows Explorer and start deleting files or subfolders in the Program Files folder, either. The proper way to uninstall a program is to remove it using the same setup program that installed it in the first place. This option should remove all traces of the program from the Registry, from the Program Files folder, and from your Start menu. Some programs include an "uninstall" or "remove" shortcut on the All Programs menu, in the same subfolder that contains other shortcuts for that program. If the program you want to remove doesn't include an uninstall shortcut, click **Start** and open Control Panel; then double-click **Add or Remove Programs**.

TIP   Use the System Restore feature to set a system checkpoint before installing or uninstalling a program. If anything goes wrong, you can roll your system configuration back to the way it was and then try again. (For step-by-step instructions on how to use System Restore, see "Create a System Restore point," page 133.)

On the left side of the Add or Remove Programs dialog box, click **Change or Remove Programs**. This displays a list of every program currently installed on your computer. Figure 1 shows one such listing. Note that the description for the highlighted program includes a link for additional information about the program, as well as an estimate of the amount of disk space the program occupies.

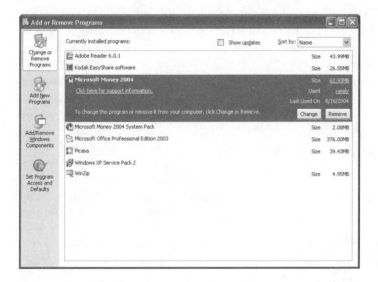

Figure 1   *This list lets you see which programs you've installed on your computer and remove those you no longer need.*

To uninstall a program, select its name in the **Currently installed programs and updates** list and then click **Remove.** To remove some components of a program without uninstalling it completely, click **Change**. In either case, follow the prompts to complete the process.

When you remove a program, Windows may ask whether you want to remove files that don't seem to be in use anymore. Usually, it's completely safe to remove any files that Windows identifies as unnecessary. If you're worried, click **No**. If you created a System Restore checkpoint before beginning the Remove operation, you can rest even easier; in the event of problems, roll back to the previous configuration, which essentially undoes your uninstall operation.

Reinstall your favorite programs

If you followed my recommendations in "Before You Begin" (page 6), this task might be a little tedious, but it shouldn't be complicated. Find the list of programs you assembled before you began setting up your new PC and begin installing them, one at a time. Start with your stack of CDs (most will run Setup automatically as soon as you insert the CD) and then work your way through the collection of programs in your Downloads folder.

As you go through this process, keep the following guidelines in mind:

- With a few exceptions, you must be logged on using an Administrator account to install programs.

- Before attempting to install a program, verify that it's compatible with Windows XP. This precaution is especially important for antivirus programs, system utilities, disk defragmenters, and other tools designed to work directly with Windows. In most of these cases, Windows XP will block the program's installation when you try to run Setup. In many cases, the error message provides a link to additional information.

- Skim through any Readme files or setup instructions to see if you need to take any special precautions (such as disabling your antivirus software or adjusting firewall settings) before running Setup.

- When installing programs you've downloaded from a Web site, look for a digital signature when you run Setup. The signature tells you the name of the program's publisher and certifies that the program hasn't been tampered with since it was signed.

CAUTION Be selective about the software you install on your new PC. A badly written program can slow down your system, cause compatibility problems, and interfere with the operation of other programs. Some programs also contain spyware or adware, which can result in unwanted pop-up windows and affect your personal privacy. When in doubt, use your favorite Web search engine to do a quick search for the program name. This simple precaution sometimes turns up horror stories and cautionary tales that may convince you to find a replacement for a program you've used for years.

CAUTION If you need to disable any security software to install a program, be sure to turn it back on as soon as setup is complete.

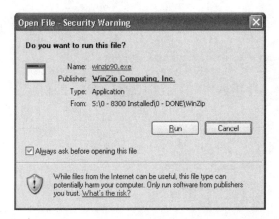

To see more details about the digital signature, click the publisher's name.

A digital signature doesn't mean a program is safe—it only means that you can verify the source of the program. You can then use that information to do additional research before deciding whether to install a program. Likewise, the absence of a digital signature doesn't mean a program is unsafe—it only means that the program's publisher didn't go through the extra step of signing the program. In that case, you might still choose to install the program. Just make sure you are confident it was created by a legitimate publisher and doesn't contain any hostile code.

● When a Setup program offers you a Custom choice, choose this option. It means a few more mouse clicks, but it also gives you the opportunity to see exactly what the Setup program is doing. You may find that some of the optional components are unnecessary or that the default settings need to be tweaked slightly for your preferences. Figure 1, for instance, shows the setup choices available when you install Apple's QuickTime software.

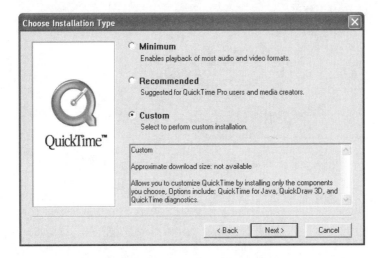

Figure 2   *When you select the Custom option, you can see what the Setup program is doing and take greater control of the process.*

● You can install some programs so that they're available for use by anyone with a user account on your computer. With most programs, however, you have to log on under each user account and run Setup again to install the program for multiple user accounts..

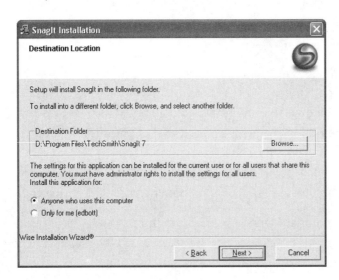

- Changes to the Windows Firewall in Service Pack 2 cause some programs to misbehave. Games and system utilities are particularly likely to fall into this category. You may need to update the software or adjust firewall settings to allow incoming connections to work properly. The software documentation should provide the details you need for this step.

- If a program requires you to enter registration information or activate it over the Internet, do so after verifying that the program starts up properly.

Update, update, update!

Over the past few years, I've noticed a dramatic increase in the number of programs that offer options to automatically check for updates. If any of your programs include this option, I highly recommend that you take advantage of it. There's no standard place to look, but you'll often find this option on the Help menu. In some cases, you need to perform this check manually. Other programs query the software publisher's Web site each time you start the program and alert you when an update is available; look on the Options or Preferences dialog box for each program to see if it offers an auto-update capability.

If you've installed Microsoft Office 2003, click **Help** and then click **Check for Updates**. This option opens Internet Explorer and takes you to the Office Online Web site (*http://office.microsoft.com*). Click **Check for Updates**. As with Windows Update, you'll first need to install a small program that scans your PC to check for required updates; from the resulting list, install the latest service packs and patches. (The Office Update site also works with Office 2000 and Office XP, but not with older Office versions.)

Organize your program shortcuts

With very few exceptions, when you install a program it creates a shortcut to the program's executable file and adds that shortcut to the All Programs menu. Getting to those shortcuts can be a tedious process, especially if the shortcut is in a subfolder of a subfolder. The solution is to reorganize the shortcuts so that they're more accessible. You can add subfolders on the All Programs menu to consolidate shortcuts; you can also create new shortcuts (or copy existing ones) and place them in more easily accessible locations. The most common locations include the top of the Start menu, the Quick Launch toolbar, and the desktop.

To work with your personal collection of program shortcuts on the All Programs menu, right-click the **Start** button and click **Open**; this allows you to work with the Start Menu folder in Windows Explorer. You'll discover that most programs place shortcuts in the All Users profile, where they're used to build the Start menu for every user account. To work with these shared shortcuts, right-click the **Start** button and click **Open All Users**.

The top of the Start menu is the logical place to add shortcuts to programs you use most frequently. Shortcuts here are prominent, easy to find, and never more than two clicks away. On a new PC, this area contains only two shortcuts, pointing to your Web browser and your e-mail program. To add a shortcut to the bottom of this list, just above the separator line, drag it from the All Programs menu or from Windows Explorer and drop it on the Start menu. The original shortcut remains where it was, and a copy appears at the top of the Start menu. (To position the shortcut in a particular place, drag its icon onto the Start button but don't release the mouse button. When the Start menu appears, drag the shortcut into position and then drop it.)

Separator line

Figure 3   *The list of shortcuts below the line changes to reflect programs you use most often. Drag a shortcut above the line to make it visible full time.*

Depending on your screen resolution, you can add approximately 7 to 10 shortcuts to the Start menu. If you prefer to have a longer list of program shortcuts available here, you can make a few tweaks to the Start menu:

1 Right-click the **Start** button and click **Properties**.

2 On the Start Menu tab, make sure **Start menu** (not **Classic Start menu**) is selected. Click **Customize**.

3 In the Customize Start Menu dialog box, make any of the following changes:

■ Click **Small Icons**. In this view, shown here on the right, you can see nearly twice as many shortcuts on the Start menu and it's easy to see that the extra shortcuts will make me much more productive. Well, maybe not...

■ Click the up or down arrows in the box to the right of **Number of programs on Start menu** to increase or decrease the number of programs on the dynamic list, below the separator line. This setting has no effect on shortcuts you add above the line.

■ Clear the check boxes to the left of **Internet** and **E-mail** to hide either or both of these standard icons. Choose a different program from the drop-down list to change the icon and menu choice if you use a different browser or e-mail program.

4 Click **OK** to save your changes.

If two clicks is one click too many, add your *favorite* favorite programs to the Quick Launch bar. This toolbar, shown here, appears just to the right of the Start button and holds icons only—no text at all, unless you hover your mouse over an icon and read the ScreenTip.

On a new installation of Windows XP, the Quick Launch bar is hidden by default. To make it visible, right-click any empty space on the taskbar (the thin space just to the right of the Start button works well). If you see a check mark on the shortcut menu to the left of **Lock the Taskbar**, click to remove it. Then click **Toolbars** and click to put a check mark next to **Quick Launch**.

You can put an unlimited number of shortcuts on the Quick Launch bar; simply drag them from the All Programs menu or from Windows Explorer. You can also rearrange the order of the shortcuts shown here. If you add more icons to the Quick Launch toolbar than Windows can show in the available space, a small arrow appears to the right of the toolbar. Click that arrow to see a pop-up menu listing the rest of the Quick Launch icons. After you're finished adding shortcuts, be sure to lock the taskbar again.

And then there's the desktop. Many programs dump shortcuts onto the desktop as part of the default setup, and lots of people are in the habit of using the desktop as a launching pad for programs. I don't recommend this strategy, because I think it makes you less productive. To find those icons on the desktop, you have to move or minimize the window you're working with, usually losing your place in whatever program is in the foreground. I prefer to keep the Windows desktop reasonably clean (in contrast to my *real* desktop, which is buried under a small mountain of paper and hardware).

Review programs that start automatically

Windows offers the capability to start programs automatically, every time you turn on your PC. Some programs take advantage of this feature during setup, creating a shortcut or Registry entry that causes the program (or some part of it) to run when you start up and remain running in the background.

You can tell Windows to add any program you want to this group by copying its shortcut into the Startup folder. Windows includes a Startup folder for your personal profile and a second Startup folder for the All Users profile.

Programs that start automatically may add a measure of convenience, but they also take a toll on performance. If you can prevent programs from auto-starting unnecessarily, you're a step ahead. Unfortunately, Windows has more than a dozen places where it can load programs so that they start up when your computer does. These places include locations buried deep in the Windows Registry. If you discover that a program is starting up automatically, and it isn't in your Startup folder, you can figure out where it's coming from by using the Windows System Configuration Utility. To work with this program, click **Start** and then click **Run**. In the Open box, type **msconfig** and press **Enter**. When the System Configuration Utility opens, click the Startup tab and you'll see a dialog box like the one shown in Figure 4.

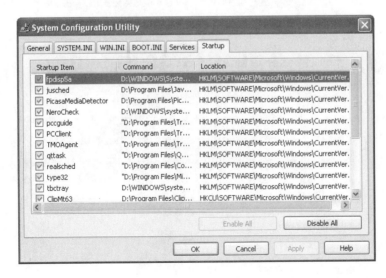

Figure 4   *Use this utility to identify names and other details of programs set to run when you start your computer.*

Sometimes it's difficult to tell exactly what program is associated with an entry in this list. For that, you may need to turn to an outside source, such as PC Pitstop (*http://www.pcpitstop.com*). If you want to get rid of a program that's in this list, open the program and find the option that prevents it from starting automatically. If you can't find that option anywhere, download a free program called Startup Control Panel (*http://www.mlin.net/StartupCPL.shtml*). After installing the program, you'll see a new Startup option in the Windows Control Panel. Use its shortcut menus to disable or delete the program, as shown in Figure 5.

Figure 5   *The Windows configuration utility can't prevent a program from starting automatically. For that, use this free third-party program.*

Get file types and programs in sync

One of the most frustrating side effects of installing software is the tendency of some programs to claim associations with types of files you want to open with another program. Programs that work with digital pictures and music files are notorious for doing this. If you install two programs that both work with digital music files, for instance, you might discover that double-clicking an MP3 file now opens that file in the second program, rather than the first one, as you intended.

This annoyance occurs because the setup routine modifies the *association* between a file type (in this case, MP3 files) and the program you installed most recently. If you notice this has happened with some file types you use regularly, try to solve the problem with one of these two options:

● **Adjust an appropriate option in the program you prefer to use.** With Windows Media Player, for instance, you can click **Tools**, and then click **Options**. On the File Types tab, click to select the check box next to the file type that another program has temporarily claimed.

● **Reinstall the program you want to use with that file type.** Sometimes all you have to do is run the Setup routine for that program again. It reclaims the file associations, and everything is well again.

If neither of these options works, you'll have to manually edit the file associations. This is the most complicated procedure, but if all else fails it's your only option.

1 Find a file of the type you want to edit, right-click the file icon in Windows Explorer, and click **Open With**.

2 If more than one program is associated with the type of file you've selected, you'll see a menu similar to the one shown here. Click **Choose Program**. (If only one program is associated with the file type you selected, you won't see a list of program choices, and you can move on to the next step.)

3 At the top of the Open With dialog box, under the **Recommended Programs** heading, Windows lists programs that are already associated with the file type you selected. All other programs installed on your computer are listed under the **Other Programs** heading.

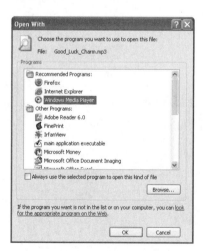

- ■ If the name of the program you want to use is in the **Recommended Programs** or **Other Programs** list, select it.

- ■ If your program isn't in this list, click **Browse**, find the executable file for that program, select it, and click **Open**.

4 Click to select the check box to the left of **Always use the selected program to open this kind of file**. Then click **OK** to save your change and close the Open With dialog box.

Set up your e-mail

If you've been using Outlook Express on your old computer, the Files and Settings Transfer Wizard should have automatically migrated your e-mail account settings, all of your messages, and your address book. (You'll need to enter the passwords for each transferred account.) If you use Microsoft Outlook, the Office Save My Settings Wizard should have accomplished the same task.

If you didn't use either wizard and you don't care about your old messages, you can set up your e-mail accounts from scratch. (As I explained in the "Before You Begin" chapter, on page 6, you'll need your account details—specifically user name, password, and the names of incoming and outgoing servers.)

The following procedure works with Outlook Express. If you use a different e-mail program, you'll need to enter the same data using the procedures that are appropriate for that program.

TIP Have you forgotten your e-mail password? See page 12 for a suggestion on how you might be able to read the hidden, saved password from your old PC.

1 Open Outlook Express. Click **Tools**, and then click **Accounts**.

2 In the Accounts dialog box, click **Add.** Click **Mail** from the shortcut menu.

3 Follow the wizard's prompts to enter the following information:

- Your display name, which appears in the From field of any message you send.

- Your e-mail address.

- Your account type: choose **POP3** for most dial-up accounts, or **HTTP** if you're setting up an MSN or Hotmail account. (The **IMAP** option represents an advanced configuration in which messages are kept on the server and you synchronize your local copy with the server. It's rarely used by consumer-oriented e-mail services.)

NOTE Do you use AOL for e-mail? Then you'll need to set up your AOL software to collect your messages. Outlook Express does not support AOL mail, nor do most other third-party e-mail programs.

■ For POP3 accounts, the names of incoming and outgoing e-mail servers.

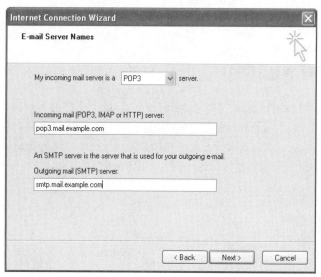

■ Your account name.

■ Your password, if you want it to be saved with your account information. Leave this field blank if you want to be prompted for your password every time you open Outlook Express and check your e-mail through this account.

If you have additional e-mail accounts, rerun the wizard to set up those accounts now. When you're finished, try sending and receiving a few messages from each account to verify that everything works properly.

Next, set up your options for automatically checking e-mail. By default, Outlook Express checks for new messages every 30 minutes. It does this automatically, as long as Outlook Express is running and you're connected to the Internet. If you have an "always on" broadband connection, you don't have to worry about checking for new messages—they just show up in your Inbox.

If your work depends on lightning-fast responses to incoming e-mail messages, you might want to check your e-mail more often—say, every 5 or 10 minutes. On the other hand, if you have a dial-up connection, you might decide to disable automatic message retrieval completely and check for new messages when you're ready to deal with them.

To set these options, open Outlook Express, click **Tools**, and then click **Options**. On the General tab of the Options dialog box shown below, review the group of settings under the **Send/Receive Messages** heading.

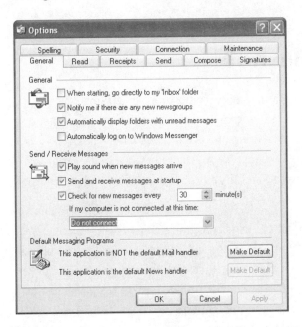

To disable automatic checks completely, clear the check box to the left of **Check for new messages every** *nn* **minutes**. To change the interval for automatic checkups, leave that box selected and either enter a new number (in minutes) or use the up and down arrows to adjust the number of minutes. You can select any number between 1 (check my e-mail every minute) and 480 (check every eight hours).

If you have a dial-up Internet account, decide whether you want Outlook Express to connect automatically when it's time to check for new messages. Choose one of the three settings under the heading **If my computer is not connected at this time**. The default setting, **Do Not Connect**, prevents Outlook Express from connecting to the Internet on its own. Choose one of the other options if you have a dedicated phone line and you're willing to allow your computer to make a connection when you're not around.

When new messages arrive, Outlook Express notifies you by playing a sound. If you get lots of e-mail messages and you've specified that you want to check for new mail every five minutes, the noise may be distracting. To turn off the notification sound, clear the check box to the left of **Play sound when new messages arrive**.

☐ Test and troubleshoot

Now that you've finished installing and configuring all your programs, give everything a good workout. Start each program and run through its main functions. Try opening some existing files and creating and editing a few new files, if possible, to confirm that it's working as you expect. Pay special attention to any programs that are critical to your work. Better to identify a problem and deal with it now than to discover a glitch in a few weeks.

In general, I advise against trying to run older programs that were originally designed for earlier versions of Windows. In some cases, Windows XP itself blocks the program's execution. If that happens to you, scratch that program off your list and start looking for a replacement. In other cases, however, the program itself may refuse to run because of a Windows version compatibility check. If the program is important to you and you are certain no update or replacement is available, you may be able to trick the program into thinking it's running under that old Windows version and it will work just fine. Here's how:

1   After installing the program, right-click its shortcut (on the All Programs menu, or on the desktop) and click **Properties**.

2   Click the Compatibility tab of the Properties dialog box, and then select the check box to the left of **Run this program in compatibility mode for:**.

3   From the drop-down list, choose the version of Windows that the program worked with previously—for most programs, this will be either Windows 95 or Windows 98/ Windows Millennium Edition (Windows Me).

4   Click **OK** to apply your changes.

When you're finished, the results should look like what's shown in Figure 6.

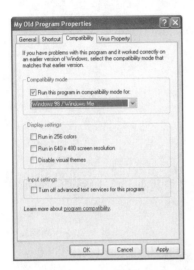

TIP   This dialog box, like others throughout Windows, includes an Apply button and an OK button. Which should you use? Click **Apply** when you want to save a change you've just made without closing the current dialog box. Click **OK** to apply the change and close the current dialog box. Click **Cancel** to close the dialog box without saving your changes.

Figure 6   *If a favorite old program won't work under Windows XP, try setting these compatibility options.*

Step 7: **Personalize and Organize**

This is the last step. In this chapter, you'll focus on the miscellaneous settings that help make using your new PC more comfortable and more productive.

If you used the Files and Settings Transfer Wizard, you may find that some of these settings already reflect the preferences you set on your old PC. Read through the entire list anyway. It won't take long, and you'll probably find a trick or two that you never knew about. If you're not sure what to choose for a particular option, feel free to skip over it. Focusing on these settings now helps you avoid annoyances later, but you can adjust most of these settings as they arise.

And don't worry about making the wrong choice. For most of the items in this chapter, you have multiple options to choose from. No two people are alike, and it's up to you to decide which arrangement is best for the way you want to use your PC.

Oh, and the part at the very end of this chapter, where I show you how to back up your data files in less than 15 minutes a week? Please do it. Honest. When (not if) you have a hard disk crash, you'll be glad you had this safety net.

☑ Checklist:

☐ **Choose your Windows style (page 174).** I recommend the Windows XP style, but you can choose the Classic style and Start menu if you prefer.

☐ **Adjust basic settings (page 176).** Tweak your display, keyboard, mouse, and other basics to make yourself more comfortable and more productive.

☐ **Give Windows Explorer a makeover (page 182).** Make file management easier by trimming clutter from Windows Explorer windows.

☐ **Fine-tune Internet Explorer and Windows Messenger (page 184).** Set your home page, customize the toolbar, and stop Messenger from starting automatically.

☐ **Spruce up your desktop (page 188).** Pick a favorite picture and use it as your desktop background, with or without icons.

☐ **Rearrange the Start menu and taskbar (page 190).** Remove the icons you don't need and show the ones you use regularly.

☐ **Customize Control Panel (page 194).** Switch between viewing by categories and seeing all available icons in an alphabetical list

☐ **Set up a screen saver (page 194).** Give yourself a little extra privacy and security—and have some fun in the process.

☐ **Create a backup and maintenance schedule (page 197).** Set up the Windows Backup program, and configure it to back up your data files every week.

Choose your Windows style

Microsoft Windows XP looks very different from older versions of Windows. For some people, in fact, it's a little *too* different. Do you want to use the distinctive Windows XP look, with its rounded corners, bright colors, and 3-D buttons? Or do you prefer the flat, not-so-flashy look of older Windows versions? You can choose the old-style look with a few clicks. Open Control Panel, click **Appearance and Themes**, and double-click **Display**. On the Appearance tab, choose **Windows Classic style** from the **Windows and buttons** list. Click **Apply** to make the change immediately without closing the dialog box, or click **OK** to make the change and close the dialog box.

Choosing the Windows Classic style does nothing more than change the appearance of Windows. But you also have a more substantive old-versus-new choice to make: Do you want to use the Windows XP–style Start menu, with its two columns? Or do you prefer the Classic Start menu, which consists of a single column, with program shortcuts at the top and settings menu options on the bottom? For a comparison, see Figure 1.

TIP   Some people who say they're turned off by the appearance of Windows XP complain about the bright colors. If that's your complaint, try choosing a different color from the **Color scheme** list on the Appearance tab. Instead of the **Default (blue)** selection, try **Silver** or **Olive green**. The silver look is particularly subtle and quite attractive.

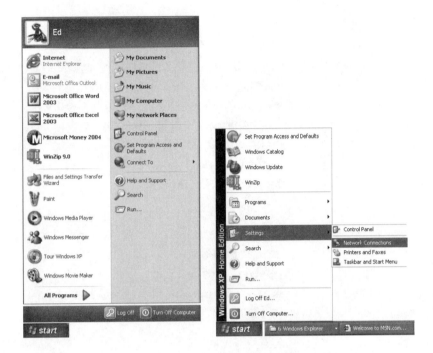

Figure 1   *If you choose the Classic Start Menu option, Windows XP replaces the new-look Start menu (left) with the original design used in older versions of Windows.*

In my opinion, the new Windows XP Start menu is much more user-friendly than the old-style (Classic) Start menu used in Windows 98, Windows Me, and Windows 2000. Give it a fair shake. If you decide you just don't like the new-fangled Start menu, you can replace it with the Classic design, which shows programs and settings in a single column. To do so, right-click the Start button, click **Properties**, click **Classic Start menu**, and click **OK**. In this chapter, I assume you're using the Windows XP interface, and I don't discuss your options for customizing the Classic Start menu configuration.

It's easy to become confused by all the options available here. Just remember that the visual settings are completely separate from the Start menu settings. You can use the two-column Windows XP–style Start menu with the old-style Windows Classic visual style, or you can use the old-style Start menu with the newer visuals.

☐ Adjust basic settings

Some parts of your new PC have a direct effect on you physically. You touch your keyboard and mouse, for example, and you stare at the display on your monitor. Take some time now to adjust these pieces of your PC. With a few little tweaks, you can make yourself more comfortable and more productive, avoid eyestrain, and even have some fun along the way. In some cases, you need to make physical adjustments to the hardware itself. For the most part, though, you make the following changes using options in the Windows Control Panel.

- **Display.** The appearance of items on your computer screen can affect your productivity and your comfort. For starters, set the screen resolution and color quality to the levels that work best for you. Right-click any empty space on the Windows desktop, and click **Properties**. (You can also get to this dialog box from Control Panel—click **Appearance and Themes** and then click **Change the screen resolution** under the **Pick a task...** heading.)

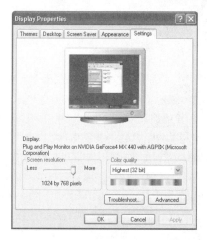

  Higher screen resolutions let you see more stuff on the screen; the trade-off is that icons and fonts appear smaller. The trick is to select the highest resolution that you can comfortably work with. For color quality, setting a higher level lets your display adapter more faithfully reproduce images; the trade-off here is with performance. On some computers, using 32-bit color quality can cause noticeable slowdowns as the screen redraws itself. If you see this happening, drop back to 16-bit color. Your eyes won't notice the difference.

Finally, physically adjust the settings on the display itself so that the screen area is centered and straight. You'll have to check the manual for your monitor or flat-panel display to see how to access these settings; typically, a button somewhere on the monitor displays an on-screen menu.

● **Keyboard and mouse.** Each of these devices has its own group of settings, which you access from Control Panel. (Click **Printers and Other Hardware** to see the Keyboard and Mouse icons.) If you've upgraded your keyboard or mouse to models that boast extra buttons and controls, you may also need to install a special software program to manage the extra settings. Pay special attention to the settings that affect mouse sensitivity; if you have trouble getting Windows to tell the difference between a single click and a double click, click the Buttons tab on the Mouse Properties dialog box and slide the **Speed control** left or right. If you use a wheel mouse, consider adjusting the settings on the Wheel tab so that each click of the wheel scrolls five or six lines (or a full screen) instead of the default three lines in Internet Explorer and Outlook Express.

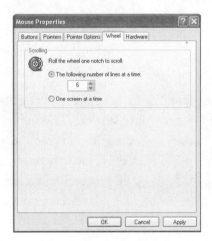

TIP I'm not a southpaw, but I have lots of lefty friends! If you use your mouse left-handed, be sure to look at the options in the Mouse Control Panel. You might want to swap the mouse buttons to make clicking more convenient.

● **Sounds.** A couple of chapters back, when you set up your hardware, you adjusted some basic sound settings, including the system volume and speaker settings. (See "Tune up your sound settings," page 145, if you want to recheck these settings now.) You also have the option at this point to adjust the specific sounds associated with system events—error messages, Windows startup, and so on. In Control Panel, click **Sounds, Speech, and Audio Devices.** Click **Change the sound scheme** to open the Sounds tab of the Sound and Audio Devices dialog box, as shown here. You can choose a ready-made collection of sounds from the **Sound scheme** list at the top of the dialog box, or go through and change the sounds for individual events by using the **Program events** and **Sounds** lists at the bottom. I don't typically change anything here.

● **Accessibility options.** If you have any physical need that affects your ability to use a PC, open Control Panel and click **Accessibility Options.** The **Cursor Options** settings shown here are particularly useful if you sometimes have trouble picking out the blinking cursor on your screen. If you're hard of hearing, you can assign visual warnings or captions to Windows sound events.

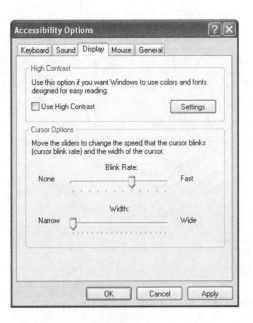

● **Date and time.** Double-click the clock at the right side of the taskbar. (This is quicker than opening the Date and Time icon from Control Panel.) Adjust the time and date, if necessary, and then click the Internet Time tab to ensure that Windows automatically updates the time. It does this using your Internet connection to check the time shown at authoritative servers. If you find that your time settings are off, try choosing **time.nist.gov** in this box; that server is managed by the United States National Institute of Standards and Technology and represents the "official" U.S. time.

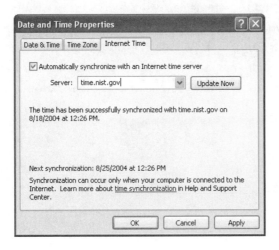

● **Power options.** Whether you have a notebook or a conventional desktop computer, you should at least check these options. They can save a little on your electric bill each month and cut down on the noise and heat your PC generates when you're not using it. Open Control Panel and double-click **Power Options**. On the Power Schemes tab, you can specify whether you want the monitor and hard disks to turn off when you're away from the PC, or whether you want the PC to go into standby mode, where it uses less power. (The dialog box shown here shows options available if you have a notebook; the **Running on batteries** options are obviously not available if you have a desktop PC.)

An even more effective way to save power is to enable hibernation. When you tell Windows that you want your PC to hibernate, it saves the entire state of your computer—which programs you're running, which files are loaded, everything—to your hard disk and shuts off the computer. When you restart, you pick up right where you left off, without having to reopen a bunch of programs and files. To turn on this feature, click the Hibernate tab and select the **Enable hibernation** check box.

CAUTION The Standby and Hibernate features are great power-saving tricks, but some hardware devices and drivers don't work properly when you switch to or from a low-power state. I recommend you test these features with your favorite programs and devices before you rely on them too extensively. Make sure you can reliably restart!

Finally, click the Advanced tab to see the options shown here. If you find the Hibernate option useful, consider choosing **Hibernate** instead of **Shut down** for the sleep or power buttons on your computer.

- **Fonts.** The Fonts folder, available from Control Panel, shows all installed fonts on your PC. To add a font to your system, drag it into this folder. If you use any custom fonts and you chose not to use the Files and Settings Transfer Wizard, you'll need to copy the font manually.

Give Windows Explorer a makeover

Windows Explorer is the program you're likely to use for most file management tasks. A long list of options is available, some of which can make Windows Explorer windows less cluttered and easier to work with. To see the full array of options, open Control Panel and double-click **Folder Options**. You're most likely to want to change options on the View tab, shown here.

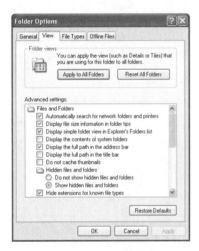

Many of the options selected here by default are appropriate for beginners or for people who don't want to see a lot of detail when using Windows Explorer. Windows experts, however, might prefer to adjust some of the following items on the **Advanced settings** list:

- **Automatically search for network folders and printers.** Disable this option if you want My Network Places to show only network shortcuts that you create manually.

- **Display simple folder view in Explorer's Folders list.** With this option on, clicking to expand the contents of a folder closes other expanded folders.

- **Hidden files and folders.** Specifies whether you want to see files that are marked as Hidden.

- **Hide extensions for known file types.** Some experts insist on disabling this option so that they can see the three-letter extensions at the end of all file names. I recommend against selecting this unless you're certain you can work with it safely. When file name extensions are enabled, you risk accidentally deleting or changing an extension, which can cause problems.

- **Hide protected operating system files (Recommended).** Clear this check box to make files that are marked with the System Attribute visible. I recommend against changing this option unless you know the operating system inside out!

- **Restore previous folder windows at logon.** If you work with projects that are organized by folders, you can specify that you want Windows to reopen whichever folders you were working with the last time you shut down.

An important part of Windows Explorer is the Recycle Bin, which allows you to recover files if you change your mind after deleting them. Right-click the Recycle Bin icon on the desktop and click **Properties**. By default, for

TIP   Do you want to keep several folder windows open at all times? Add shortcuts to those folders to your Startup group and they'll be opened automatically each time you log on to your account.

instance, Windows asks you to confirm your action each time you delete a file. I find those dialog boxes annoying, so I make sure to clear the **Display delete confirmation dialog** check box here. I advise against clicking the **Do not move files to the Recycle Bin** box, however. Doing so leaves you without this important safety net and unable to recover a file if you accidentally delete it!

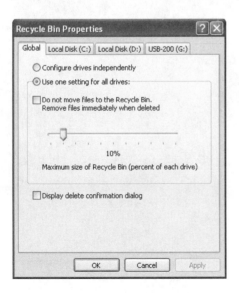

Fine-tune Internet Explorer and Windows Messenger

In "Step 2: Protect Your PC," I explained how to enable Internet Explorer's pop-up blocker and cookie management features. (If you want to check these settings again, see page 79.) Here, you can check and, if necessary, change some settings that affect the way Internet Explorer looks and acts. Some of these settings are strictly for experts, but others are useful for just about anyone.

Start by setting your home page. Open Internet Explorer and go to the Web page you want to use as your home page—the one that appears whenever you open a new Internet Explorer window. Click **Tools**, and then click **Internet Options**. On the General tab, check to make sure your selected home page is listed; if you see another page (such as *http://www.msn.com*) listed instead, click **Use Current** in the **Home page** section.

Next, adjust the size of the Internet Explorer cache. Under the **Temporary Internet Files** heading, click **Settings....** If you have a big hard disk, the value in the **Amount of disk space to use** box may be very large. You can safely set it to 100 MB or less. Don't change any other settings in this dialog box.

Finally, click the Advanced tab, where you'll find a long list of mostly esoteric settings. Go through the list, paying special attention to these settings:

- **Disable Script Debugging.** Both of these options should be selected to prevent you from being pestered by annoying dialog boxes when you visit a Web page that includes a bad piece of script. There's nothing you can do about someone else's pages, so why should you try to debug them?

- **Enable page transitions.** Clear this check box if you want to prevent Internet Explorer from showing transitions such as fading in or out.

- **Enable Personalized Favorites Menu.** If this check box is selected, your Favorites list hides menu items you haven't used lately. I recommend that you not select this box, because the result is more confusing than helpful.

- **Enable third-party browser extensions.** Clear this check box if you want to lessen the chance of being attacked by spyware. You will also lose the ability to install helpful updates as well.

- **Notify when downloads complete.** When you download a program or other file from a Web site, you see a status dialog box as it downloads. When the file is downloaded, this dialog box remains open and displays a button that allows you to open the folder containing the downloaded file.

- **Search from the Address bar.** Choose one of the four options here to determine what happens when you enter search text instead of a URL in the Address bar. I prefer the **Display results, and go to the most likely site** option.

- **Security.** You can override some basic security measures in Inter Explorer here, such as allowing downloaded software to install even with an invalid digital signature. Unless you're a security expert, I highly recommend not touching any options here.

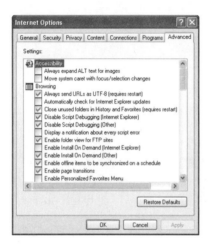

You can also customize the Internet Explorer toolbars. Click **View**, then click **Toolbars**, and click the name of any available toolbar to show or hide it (a check mark means it's currently visible). To customize the Standard toolbar, click **View** and then click **Customize**. This dialog box gives you several ways to change the appearance of this toolbar, as shown in Figure 2.

I like to switch to the **Small icons** option with **Selective text on right**, which uses a little less space. I also like to customize the lineup of buttons. To add a button, click its entry in the **Available toolbar buttons list** and click **Add**. I don't need the Discuss button, so I select its entry in the **Current toolbar buttons** list and click **Remove**. To change a button's position, click its entry in this list and then click **Move Up** or **Move Down**.

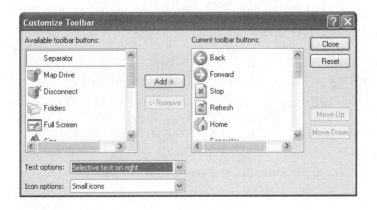

Figure 2 *Use these options to make the Internet Explorer toolbar smaller or change the arrangement of buttons there.*

If you use Windows Messenger or MSN Messenger for online chats, you can enable them to log on using your Passport automatically. If you don't use Windows Messenger, or if you use it only occasionally and don't want it running all the time, you might find it annoying that it starts automatically. Here's how to disable it:

1 Click **Start**, click **All Programs**, and then click **Windows Messenger**.

2 From the Messenger window, click **Tools**, and then click **Options**.

3 On the Preferences tab, clear the top two options, **Run Windows Messenger when Windows starts** and **Allow Windows Messenger to run in the background**.

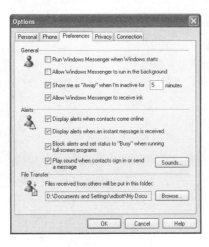

4   If you use Outlook Express or Microsoft Outlook, you'll need to clear a matching option in either or both of these programs:

- Open Outlook Express, click **Tools**, click **Options**, click the General tab, and clear the check box to the left of **Automatically log on to Windows Messenger**. Then click **View**, click **Layout**, and clear the **Contacts** check box.

- Open Microsoft Outlook, click **Tools**, click **Options**, and then click the Other tab. Under the **Person Names** heading, clear **Enable Person Names Smart Tag** and **Display Messenger Status in the From field**.

☐ Spruce up your desktop

How boring is your desktop? Your new PC may use the dreamy Bliss background that comes with Windows XP (a green field and a blue sky filled with fluffy clouds), or the company that made your PC may have installed some form of its logo as wallpaper. Either way, wouldn't you rather use something a little more personal as your desktop background?

Right-click any empty space on the Windows desktop, and click **Properties**. On the Desktop tab, scroll through the selections in the **Background** list and see if something strikes your fancy. If you can't find a suitable image there, click **Browse** and choose a digital image from your My Pictures folder.

The perfect image, of course, is one that fits your screen resolution perfectly. So, if you have set your screen resolution to 1024 × 768, a picture with the same dimensions will cover every pixel on the screen without any cropping. In practice, pictures you take are unlikely to be just the right size. If you're handy with an image-editing program (and if you're also a bit obsessed about little details like this), you can pick a picture and crop it to the right size. If that seems like too much trouble, pick an image of approximately the right size and use one of the three options on the **Position** menu:

- **Stretch** This choice, as you might guess, forces the image you selected to fit in the available desktop space. If the image is too large, it gets squished down. For a picture with a horizontal orientation roughly similar to your PC's display, you can get away with some stretching or shrinking; however, if the shape is too different, the result can look distorted

- **Center** This choice places the center of the image you selected in the center of the screen. If the image is too big to fit either vertically or horizontally, the portions that are outside the screen dimensions are cropped out. If either dimension is smaller than the screen resolution, you see a blank space on the top and bottom or the left and right sides. This choice works well for images that are smaller than the screen; you get a nice "framing" effect and can place desktop icons on the blank portion.

- **Tile** This choice repeats your image as many times as it will fit in the current screen resolution. It is the best choice when you have a small image (like a postage stamp) that you want to use as a pattern.

I change my background image all the time. Although you can use the Display Properties dialog box, as shown here, it's much faster to open My Pictures, right-click the picture you want to use as your background, and click **Set as desktop background**.

TIP If you want to go completely gaga with background images, sounds, cursors, and other flashy stuff, pick up a copy of Microsoft Plus! for Windows XP. This add-on package includes custom themes, screen savers, and games. More details are available at *http://www.microsoft.com/windows/plus*.

Are you wondering where the icons on your desktop went? Unlike previous versions, Windows XP uses a clean desktop without the icons found on the desktop in earlier Windows versions. Personally, I rarely use the desktop as a starting point for anything, so I like this clutter-free approach. But if you would rather have the My Documents or My Computer icon on the desktop, click **Customize Desktop** on the Desktop tab of the Display Properties dialog box. This is where you can decide which icons you want on your desktop. Click to select the check box for any icons you want to make visible.

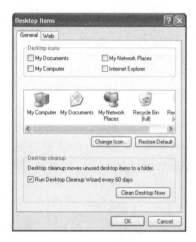

Rearrange the Start menu and taskbar

The Windows XP Start menu consists of two columns. You already customized the contents of the left column (if you want to run through this procedure again, see "Organize your program shortcuts," page 159). In this section, I'll show you how to customize the right column so it includes the exact arrangement of icons you want to keep close at hand.

This column is divided into three groups. You can go through a list of menu items and add or remove icons from the menu (although you cannot change the order in which they appear on the menu). You can also customize the way these menus behave. Here's how:

1 Right-click the Start button and click **Properties**.

2 On the Start Menu tab, ensure that **Start menu** is selected and then click **Customize**.

3 Click the Advanced tab of the Customize Start Menu dialog box, and then adjust the following options under **Start menu settings**:

NOTE If **Classic Start menu** is selected, an entirely different set of options appears and you don't have a second column to work with.

- **Open submenus when I pause on them with my mouse** Clear this check box if you prefer to click to open submenus rather than having them fly out on their own.

- **Highlight newly installed programs** Normally, when you install a new program, its entry on the All Programs menu is highlighted. Clear this check box if you don't want this behavior to occur.

4 Go through the list in the **Start menu items** box. This list, for some strange reason, is in alphabetical order, and its sheer length might seem intimidating. But go through it in groups and you'll find the task a little easier:

- Items that can be displayed as a link, as a menu, or not at all: **Control Panel, My Computer, My Documents, My Music, My Pictures, Network Connections**. When you click the **Display as a menu** option, clicking the icon results in a menu that flies out to the right. This works well for the Network Connections folder but can be overwhelming for folders that are filled with lots of files.

■ Items that can be displayed as links or hidden: **Favorites menu, Help and Support, My Network Places, Printers & Faxes, Run command, Search, Set Program Access and Defaults**. Select or clear the appropriate check box. I recommend that you not hide Help and Support or the Run command.

■ **System Administrative Tools** can be displayed on the All Programs menu, on the Start menu, or not at all. If you're a Windows expert, it's handy to have these tools readily available.

■ Finally, two options allow you to adjust Start menu behavior: **Enable dragging and dropping** lets you add or remove items from the Start menu with the mouse, and **Scroll Programs** controls how the All Programs menu works when you add more items than will fit on a single screen.

5 Decide whether you want to display the My Recent Documents menu. This option keeps track of data files you open from Windows Explorer; to eliminate it, clear the check box to the left of **List my most recently opened documents**.

6 Click **OK** to save your changes.

Now go back to the Taskbar and Start Menu Properties dialog box and click the Taskbar tab. This dialog box includes the following options that affect how the taskbar behaves. The following options are available under the **Taskbar appearance** heading:

● **Lock the taskbar** This option is also available if you right-click any empty space on the taskbar. After you get everything arranged just right, click this check box to make sure you don't accidentally make any changes.

● **Auto-hide the taskbar** This option causes the taskbar to slide down and out of the way when you're working elsewhere. It reappears if you "bump" the mouse pointer on the bottom of the screen. Some people like this option because it gives you a little extra screen room, but I find it too confusing and hard to deal with.

- **Keep the taskbar on top of other windows** This option should remain on. If you clear the check box, any window you maximize will cover the taskbar.

- **Group similar taskbar buttons** In Windows XP, when you have more windows open than you have room for on the taskbar, windows from the same program get grouped under a single button. I find this a really great way to work with lots of windows, but other people find it confusing. Take your pick.

- **Show Quick Launch** This is a great place to put shortcuts to your most favorite programs. For an explanation of how this toolbar works, see "Organize your program shortcuts," page 159.

Under the **Notification area** heading, click **Customize** to tweak the icons that appear in the tray at the right of the taskbar. Most of the time, Windows does a good job of hiding the icons you don't need and showing the ones you do use. But if you find some icons are popping up when you don't need them and others are mysteriously AWOL, you can change the settings here. For each icon, you have three choices: **Always hide**, **Always show**, or **Hide when inactive**.

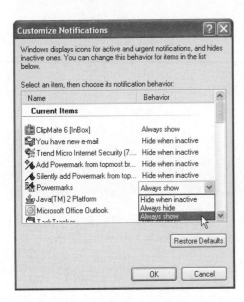

Customize Control Panel

Throughout this book, we've used Control Panel extensively, and you'll use it many more times in the future as you continue to work with your PC. The one and only option in Control Panel determines whether you want to view the icons by category or as a single folder full of individual icons. In my experience, Windows experts tend to like the single alphabetical list, and folks with a more casual attitude toward computers prefer the categorical view. You can switch to the icons view by clicking **Switch to Classic View** under the **Control Panel** heading in the tasks pane on the left. Click **Switch to Category View** to change back.

Set up a screen saver

Let's get one thing clear right up front: Screen savers don't really save your screen. Oh, sure, they *used* to, back in the prehistoric era of personal computing. But these days the main reason to use a screen saver is security, with entertainment a close second.

Screen savers work by monitoring your keyboard and mouse. After a period of time passes with no keystrokes or clicks, the screen saver kicks in and replaces the contents of your screen with an interesting image. This protects your privacy by preventing a passer-by from seeing what you're working on. In Windows XP, screen savers typically include the option to require that you log on with your password when you move the mouse or touch a key. This is a very effective security precaution.

To set up one of the Windows XP screen savers, right-click any empty space on the desktop, click **Properties**, and click the Screen Saver tab on the Display Properties dialog box.

The **Screen saver** list includes an assortment of geometric shapes, text, and graphics that swoosh, zoom, and dart about the screen. When you choose an item from this list, a small preview appears in the dialog box itself. Click **Preview** to see what the screen saver looks like in action; move the mouse or tap a key to return to this dialog box.

Use the **Wait _nn_ minutes** box to specify how long you want the screen saver to wait before it springs into action. Be sure to make this interval long enough that you won't be interrupted when you take a two-minute break, but short enough to activate when you step away from your desk. The default of 10 minutes should be good for most people. If you also want to password-protect your screen, click **On resume, display Welcome screen**.

After you've selected a screen saver, click **Settings** to see additional options that may be available for that choice. In general, you can choose the speed of the effect as well as certain display characteristics (such as the number of pipes and surface style for the 3D Pipes screen saver).

One of my favorite screen savers is the My Pictures Slideshow. This option pulls
pictures at random from your My Pictures folder, slides them onto the screen using
an assortment of interesting transition effects, and leaves each picture visible for a
period ranging from 6 seconds to 3 minutes. Click **Settings** to specify that you want
to restrict this screen saver to a particular folder. You can then select your most
screen-worthy pictures, put copies in this folder, and have only these pictures cycle
through when the screen saver runs.

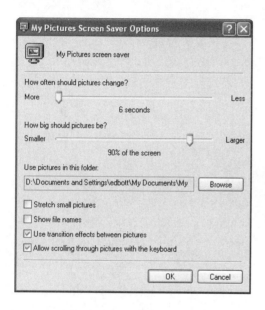

Create a backup and maintenance schedule

This is the final task in setting up your new PC. In many respects, it's the most important. You've just organized all your personal data. You've configured Windows so that it's running just the way you like it. All your programs are up to date. It's time to create a backup schedule and perform your first backup.

Yes, I know. Backing up is tedious work, and it's easy to find excuses to avoid it. But a regular backup takes just a few minutes a week (about 15 minutes for each gigabyte of data), and you'll thank me when you need those backed-up files. Think you're immune? Think again. Hard disks crash. A direct lightning strike can fry your computer's innards. A virus might sneak past your defenses. When (not if, but when) one of those dire events happens, you'll be grateful you had your important data files backed up and stored in a safe place.

To reliably back up your data files, you need three things:

- **Backup software.** Windows XP includes an excellent backup program. You can also purchase third-party programs specifically designed for Windows XP.

- **A place to store your backed-up files.** If you don't have a lot of data, you might be able to get by with a Zip drive and a handful of Zip disks (each one holds either 100 MB or 250 MB). If you have a big collection of digital photos and music, you'll need a much bigger backup destination. I recommend that you get an external hard drive that plugs into a high-speed USB 2.0 or FireWire port. If you have a fast Internet connection, consider subscribing to Xdrive (*http://www.xdrive.com*) or @Backup (*http://www.backup.com*), where you can store files on a remote server specifically designed for this purpose.

> **TIP** If you have a CD burner with a program like DirectCD or InCD installed, you can save your backup files directly to a CD. If you have a DVD burner, save the backup set to a file on your hard drive and then copy it to a DVD, which can hold more than 4 GB of data.

- **A regular backup schedule.** I've created a Scheduled Task that automatically backs up all my data files every Friday afternoon. I'll show you how to do the same.

Where is the Windows XP Backup program? That depends on which edition of Windows XP you have installed.

- If you have Windows XP Professional, the Backup program is installed automatically along with Windows.

- If you have Windows XP Home Edition, the Backup program is available on the CD, but you have to install it yourself. To do so, insert the Windows XP CD into your CD-ROM drive and open a Windows Explorer window showing the contents of the CD. Double-click the Valueadd folder, then the Msft folder, and finally the Ntbackup folder. Click the Ntbackup icon to install the Backup program.

To begin working with the Backup program, click **Start**, click **All Programs**; then click **Accessories**, click **System Tools**, and (finally!) click the **Backup** shortcut. The Backup program uses an easy-to-follow wizard to walk you through the process of backing up. In this example, I assume you're using the Windows Backup program with an external hard drive.

1 Click **Next** to skip past the Welcome page.

2 On the **Backup or Restore** page, click **Back up files and settings** and click **Next**.

3 On the **What to Back Up** page, select one of the following four options and click **Next**:

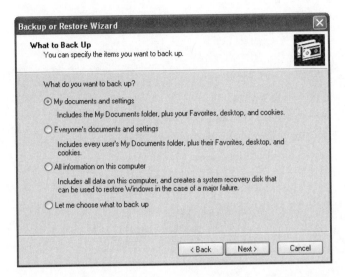

- **My documents and settings** Choose this option if you just want to back up your personal files. This is the option I recommend for most people.

- **Everyone's documents and settings** Choose this option if your computer has several user accounts and you're responsible for backing up the data files for every user.

- **All information on this computer** This option is the perfect way to back up everything on your PC—programs, settings, and data. It's the right choice only if you have a storage device (such as an external hard disk) that is at least as big as your main hard disk.

- **Let me choose what to back up** If you need to back up data files stored on another computer on your network, select this option.

4 On the **Backup Type, Destination, and Name** page, choose the place where you want to save your backed-up files and settings. The drop-down list shows all removable drives (floppy and Zip drives, for instance). To select an external hard disk, click **Browse...** and select the drive letter and folder where you want your backup files to go. In the **Type a name for this backup** box, enter a descriptive name for the file that will contain your backed-up data. Click **Next** to continue.

NOTE The options in the **Select the backup type** list at the top of this dialog box are available only if you have a backup tape drive installed. If you have no tape drive, the File backup type is selected and cannot be changed.

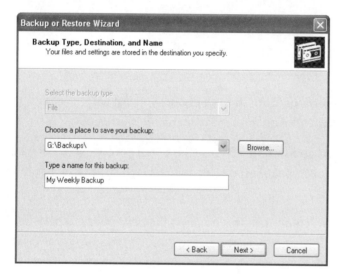

5 On the final page, the wizard displays a summary of the settings you chose in the previous pages. Don't click **Finish** just yet. Instead, click **Advanced**, where you'll find the option to perform a backup automatically.

6 Click **Next** twice to move past the **Type of Backup** and **How to Back Up** pages. On the **Backup Options** page, click **Replace the existing backups** and click **Next**.

7 On the **When to Back Up** page, click **Later**, enter a descriptive name in the **Job name box,** and click **Set Schedule**.

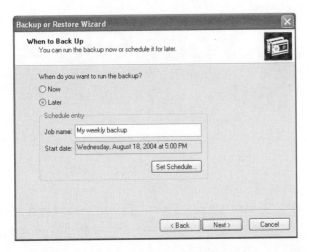

8 On the **Schedule Job** dialog box, set the options as shown here to perform a weekly
backup every Friday at 5:00 PM. (Feel free to experiment with different options.)
Click **OK** to save your scheduled task, enter your user name and password when
prompted, and click **Next.**

9 Review the settings on the **Completing the Backup or Restore Wizard** page. If
they're correct, click **Finish** to save the scheduled backup.

Make sure your backup drive is powered on and connected to your computer. For
the first few weeks, check the backed-up files carefully and make sure that
everything you want to back up is getting saved.

And that's it. Your new PC is all ready to go. In the final chapter, I'll help you figure
out what to do with your old PC.

Clean Up Your Old Computer

Your new PC is ready for duty. So what are you planning to do with your old computer? Hand it down? Give it to charity? Throw it in the trash? Before you decide, take a few minutes to review your options.

Privacy and security, of course, should be your primary concerns. The hard disk in your old computer is probably packed with personal and financial details that could cost you dearly if they fell into unscrupulous hands. If you think you have nothing worth stealing, you might be surprised, especially if you've ever purchased products online or checked your bank balance via the Web. I'll show you how to wipe out the traces of your old data so you can reduce the chances that you'll have your credit card compromised or your identity stolen.

Giving a computer away is a noble thought—if you can find someone willing to take it off your hands. That might not be as easy as it sounds, especially if your creaky old PC is more than three or four years old.

If you conclude that your old PC has reached the end of the road, don't just toss it in the trash bin. Some of its components are toxic, and others are recyclable. Doing the right thing for the planet means finding someone who will dispose of those old PC pieces in the right places. You'll find some useful pointers in this chapter.

Know your options

What is your old computer worth? Forget how much you paid for it originally—computer hardware depreciates faster than just about any consumer product you can think of, including cars. In my experience, every year of a computer's existence is equivalent to about three years' wear and tear on a car. If you've squeezed five years' of productive use from your computer, it might be worth a lot less than you think. Your options include the following:

- **Give it away or sell it.** Most schools and charities have minimum requirements for PC hardware; this is especially true of schools. Larger charities like the National Cristina Foundation (*http://www.cristina.org*) are a little more forgiving.

- **Reuse it in your own home or office.** That old PC is no longer fast enough to serve as your primary computer, but it might have enough oomph to handle occasional Web browsing or light word processing. You can extend its life with a few well-chosen upgrades.

- **Cannibalize it for spare parts.** You might be able to get some extra mileage from the memory chips, hard drive, or video card in your old computer. If you can't use the salvaged parts, you might know someone who can.

- **Recycle!** Check with mail-order computer suppliers, local electronics stores, and your local government—chances are someone can help you.

Prepare your old PC for a new home

If you've determined that your old computer has some life left in it, you might want to consider some upgrades. Most people don't realize that the least important component of a PC is its processor chip. Add a big enough hard disk, some extra memory, and a fresh copy of Windows XP, and you may be surprised at how zippy that old computer becomes. (If you try to pawn it off on the kids, however, they will point out how thoroughly inadequate it is for playing games. And they will be right.)

To determine what sort of hardware is currently installed in your old PC, download the Belarc Advisor, a free utility available from *http://www.belarc.com*. It takes seconds to run and tells you exactly what's included in your old PC. If your old PC meets at least the following standards, it is a candidate for an upgrade to Windows XP:

- **CPU:** minimum 366 MHz (preferably 500 MHz or better)

- **Memory:** at least 128MB (preferably 256 MB or more)

- **Hard drive:** at least 20 GB (preferably 40 GB or more)

If your computer falls short in terms of memory or hard drive space, you may find it worth your while to upgrade. Upgrades typically make the most sense if you can perform the installation yourself or convince a tech-savvy friend to help you for free. If your computer can't be upgraded to support Windows XP, find the original operating system disks and get ready to reinstall your old version of Windows.

What about the software on your old PC? Check the license agreement included with each program. If you've moved a program to your new PC, the terms of the license agreement may require you to erase it from your old PC. If you plan to donate the computer to a charitable organization or school, they'll typically ask for physical copies of the software licenses along with your signed agreement to transfer those licenses.

Erase your old data...completely

Data has a way of sticking around long after it should be gone. Traces of your identity, including passwords and personal information, can be saved in temporary files on your hard disk. If you wipe out the contents of the folders where you normally store data, you may inadvertently overlook these other, hidden files. And even when you delete a file from your hard disk, it doesn't really go away. The bits remain on the hard disk until they're physically overwritten by other data. With simple disk utilities, anyone can recover files or snippets of data from files that were supposedly erased.

If you're just moving your computer upstairs for the kids to use, you might decide that wiping every bit of data from your hard drive is overkill. Fair enough. But if your computer is destined for points unknown, like a charity or the town dump, you owe it to yourself to wipe it clean first.

There are literally dozens of utilities that can do this job for you. Most work the same way, by repeatedly writing random bits to all parts of your disk where files have been stored, and then wiping those bits away. When the process is complete, you'd need one of those super-secret government spy agencies to recover any of the data that used to be there. Use your favorite search engine to look for **disk wiping utilities for windows**. Some are free, some are relatively inexpensive shareware, and others are full-fledged commercial programs.

After you've wiped the hard disk completely clean, you can reinstall your old operating system or upgrade to Windows XP.

⬜ Recycle your old PC responsibly

What if you decide your old PC is junk? Please don't just throw it in the trash. Instead, recover what you can, and then recycle the remainder in a responsible way. You may be able to use your old hard disk as a secondary drive in the new PC. Likewise, the memory chips, video card, network adapter, keyboard, and mouse may have value as spare parts.

After you've removed anything worthwhile, find a safe place to dump the remainder of the PC. Check with whoever runs your local waste disposal facility. Where I live, the city holds recycling fairs every few months where they accept old consumer electronics products and computers for recycling and disposal. Keep those unwanted pieces of your PC in the garage until the next opportunity to dispose of them the right way.

Some computer manufacturers will take your old PC, regardless of who manufactured it and what condition it's in. They typically send all these pieces to a firm that disassembles the pieces and recycles them. Among mail-order manufacturers, Dell and Gateway have developed excellent recycling programs. Among firms with retails stores, check out Best Buy and Office Depot, both of which allow customers to drop off old computers, cell phones, and consumer electronics devices for recycling.

And that's it. Your new PC is all set up, your old PC has found a new home, and you're ready to get to work (or play). Enjoy!

Index

Ed Bott is a best-selling author and award-winning journalist who has been writing about personal computers for nearly two decades. His friendly, easy-to-follow style and mastery of Windows, in titles such as *Faster Smarter Windows XP* and *Windows XP Inside Out*, have earned a loyal following among beginners and power users alike. Ed was previously editor of *PC Computing* and managing editor of *PC World*. He and his wife Judy live in the sunny Southwest with their two amazingly smart and affectionate cats, Katy and Bianca.

What do you think of this book? We want to hear from you!

Do you have a few minutes to participate in a brief online survey? Microsoft is interested in hearing your feedback about this publication so that we can continually improve our books and learning resources for you.

To participate in our survey, please visit:

www.microsoft.com/learning/booksurvey

And enter this book's ISBN, 0-7356-2117-9. As a thank-you to survey participants in the United States and Canada, each month we'll randomly select five respondents to win one of five $100 gift certificates from a leading online merchant.* At the conclusion of the survey, you can enter the drawing by providing your e-mail address, which will be used for prize notification *only*.

Thanks in advance for your input. Your opinion counts!

Sincerely,

Microsoft® Learning

Learn More. Go Further.